We are,
at the time I
write this, in need of
a revolution in
education

This is a strong statement
and I don't use it lightly

Teaching: notes from the front line

Dr Debra Kidd

 Independent Thinking Press

All royalties from this book will go to the Big i Foundation –
helping children in their fight for the right to study

www.independentthinking.co.uk/info/big-i-foundation

First published by

Independent Thinking Press
Crown Buildings, Bancyfelin, Carmarthen, Wales, SA33 5ND, UK
www.independentthinkingpress.com

Independent Thinking Press is an imprint of Crown House Publishing Ltd.

Edited by Ian Gilbert

British Library Cataloguing-in-Publication Data

A catalogue entry for this book is available from the British Library.

Print ISBN 978-1-78135-131-4
Mobi ISBN 978-1-78135-193-2
ePub ISBN 978-1-78165-194-9
ePDF ISBN 978-1-78135-195-6

Printed and bound in the UK by
Gomer Press, Llandysul, Ceredigion

To Florence and Chris Ridehalgh, my mum and dad. For bringing home boxes of books from charity shops when you were too poor to buy new. For making me learn 'proper' spellings while I was being taught ITA. For all those years of birthdays sitting on the end of my bed and telling me, 'This will be the most important year of your life – work hard.' It became a joke, but it stuck. For making me argumentative and nowty. For loving and supporting me even though I am argumentative and nowty. I love you both.

Read not to contradict and confute; nor to believe and take for granted; nor to find talk and discourse; but to weigh and consider.

Francis Bacon, *Of Empire* **(1625)**

CONTENTS

Introduction 1

1 Dead Man's Clothing 9

2 The Future: Run or Ride? 27

3 Neo-Narcissism: The Problem with
   International Comparisons 43

4 The Game of Clones: Ofsted and Accountability 59

5 Teaching: Not for Lily Pad Hoppers 79

6 Moo Cows in Showers: Celebrating Complexity 99

7 (R)evolution: Pedagogical Activism 111

Bibliography *121*

Introduction

For though I am not splenitive and rash,

Yet have I in me something dangerous,

Which let thy wisdom fear.

Shakespeare, *Hamlet*, Act 5, Scene 1

I used to quite enjoy physics in Year 9. We'd arrive at our lesson, collect a textbook from the teacher's desk and turn to whatever page he'd written on the blackboard. And then, while he sat on the steps of the fire escape with a newspaper, cigarette and a cup of coffee, we'd discuss the Burnley game from the night before. I didn't learn any physics, of course, but I learned a lot about football and found out that if you were a girl who knew about football you were quite interesting to boys. I don't think that is what our teacher had hoped for. But then I don't think he had hopes for us at all in that school, which was in its first year of comprehensive status, having been a secondary modern for years. I don't think he was used to giving children hope and joy. I think about those lessons a lot when people talk about how the quality of education has deteriorated over the past four or five decades. I wonder where they went to school because, among my peer group, my experience was not unusual.

When I left my secondary school at 16 clutching a handful of O levels, my dad sent me to a private school. It was his way of feeling that he was providing the 'best' for his daughter, having spent years painstakingly building up a business and carrying his family out of poverty into an affluence symbolised by bidets, Volvos and independent education.

With the exception of two teachers who seemed to think that discussing things was useful, our lessons largely consisted of taking notes from a teacher/reader sitting at a desk dictating from a book. It seemed that money bought compliant classmates but little in the way of teaching quality. No one took responsibility for our results. You listened, took notes, memorised and regurgitated. And if you did this successfully, and were able to respond succinctly to fairly predictable questions, you passed your A levels. It was as easy as that. Hardly anyone did A levels then, so there were plenty of university places to go around and you didn't have to stress about grades too much. One grade B and a couple of Cs would get you through the door of a Russell Group university. Simple. And if you failed? Well, that was your fault, nobody else's.

Was it really that bad in both settings? Of course not. In the first, there was the wonderful Dorothy Bowling who encouraged in me a lifelong love of music, and in the second, the witty Dave Hopkinson who made me see the importance of politics. Both brought interests into my life that enriched and influenced my future, as teachers have done for children throughout time. But back then there was a great deal of inconsistency, and this inconsistency was a national problem.

There is little doubt that when education began to rise in political prominence during the 1980s – a priority which rose as manufacturing industries declined – teaching practice was so patchy across the country that some structure was necessary. The quality of teaching and learning could not be left to chance. There was a need for national standards and forms of accountability – no one who remembers education in the 1970s and 1980s can argue with that. But, unfortunately, instead of exploring how the very best and most successful practice could be shared, instead of looking at what we could learn about pedagogy, education became a vehicle for pushing forward political agendas in order to win votes. In his comprehensive book, *Thinking Allowed on Schooling*, Mick Waters takes us through an entertaining guide of how each education minister has, over the years, tried to become associated with one forgotten initiative after another in order to make their mark.[1] It would be funny if this had not come hand in hand with accusations that teachers, children and parents were consistently failing. As a result, we teachers have become accustomed to hearing and absorbing rhetoric about 'falling standards', 'unacceptable failures' and even 'cheating'. We have been told so many times that we are not worthy of trust that we have begun to turn on each other. We have allowed ourselves to be beaten down into an acceptance of the belief that we cannot be trusted to form our own policies and practices and that we are in need not only of guidance but policing. We have begun to believe that if we do what we're told, we will be rewarded and win acceptance. We beg to be 'outstanding'; we crave affirmation.

These needs are managed and fed by people whose interests are served by developing tightly controlled monitoring and micro-management systems, individuals who can take the credit for any perceived success: politicians, consultants, advisers. It forms part of a myth of decline, which allows economic reform to dictate education policy without challenge from voting parents.[2] Who is going to argue with a politician who promises to make their child's school 'better'? As teachers, we take this relentless, critical interference

----

1 Mick Waters, *Thinking Allowed on Schooling* (Carmarthen, Independent Thinking Press, 2013), pp. 55–58.

2 Stephen Ball, *The Education Debate*, 2nd edn (Bristol: Policy Press, 2012), pp. 11–16.

from people who rarely understand the complexities of classroom interactions or the difficulties of balancing all the competing needs of children, paperwork and parental expectations. We have become de-professionalised, uncertain and afraid. We have begun to believe that we are not good enough, when, in fact, even Ofsted concedes that the teaching profession is the best it has ever been. It is time to take our vocation back, to learn to trust ourselves and each other and, crucially, to take control of the direction of education and policy.

This is a book about redirecting, rechanneling and reaffirming; about taking positive action. It challenges the overpowering but deadening desire for certainty that has formed the illusion that data is truth. And because I am a teacher, and because this book is about being a teacher and taking control, it is about activism both in and out of the classroom. It is activism informed by knowledge *and* practice, fuelled by networking, reading and collaborating. It is the activism of experience gained inside the classroom in the day-to-day interactions with children. It is pedagogical activism.

We are, at the time I write this, in need of a revolution in education. This is a strong statement and I don't use it lightly. And I am not alone in calling for it. At the Festival of Education in 2013, Charles Leadbeater used an example from aeronautical engineering to try to explain what was happening in education.[3] He showed a picture of the Douglas DC-3 – the aircraft of choice in the 1950s. The problem with the DC-3 was that it flew at an altitude that meant it had to fly through cloud cover, leading to many cancelled flights and constant damage to the aircraft. While

---

3   Charles Leadbeater, Technology in Education: The Past, Present and Future. Speech delivered at the *Sunday Times* Festival of Education, Wellington College, Berkshire, 21–22 June 2013.

technology was beginning to be available to design planes which could fly at higher altitudes – above the clouds – most airlines preferred to continue tinkering with and improving the DC-3. Eventually, an airline invested in Boeing planes and the rest is history. Leadbeater described Michael Gove as a passionate engineer of the DC-3, desperately battling to keep his favourite craft in the air, while convincing passengers that the Boeing would fail. Leadbeater argued for 'regime change', urging parents and teachers to overcome the 'cartel of fear' that keeps the 'DC-3' in operation – the fear of the unknown and the worry that change will be bad. But doing nothing is worse.

Our current education system is overloaded with amendments, additions and adjustments which have been designed to keep an outdated model in the air. But it is crashing. And as it comes down, we see the battle of blame begin. It is presented to us as a battle between traditional and progressive methods when, in fact, the vast majority of teachers steer a pathway through the middle. It is presented as a battle for the future success of our nation, built on rhetoric from the past. It is a battle being fought at the extremes where both language and actions are dangerous. It is a battleground on which politicians think it is justifiable to change examination syllabi and criteria halfway through a course in order to appear 'tough'. A place where teachers working to ensure the best possible chances of success for children are labelled as 'cheats'. This is a moral no-man's-land where immediate changes to education are announced on television and in newspapers rather than through the examination regulators and boards. We are in a mêlée where politicians behave like schoolboys; dumping their girlfriends by text message and spreading gossip about them to justify the rudeness. We are living through a time when expertise is ignored, opposition is dismissed and ridiculed and where anyone with an alternative view is labelled an 'enemy of promise'.[4] These are dark times, indeed, but the darkness has been creeping up for many years and the night will be long, unless teachers take action.

When under pressure, it's easy to look for those who are to blame. There is no doubt, as I will explore in this book, that politicians of all colours have a lot to answer for. But this would be an oversimplification of the situation. We need to look closer to home if we are to really change the way things are. How many of us have quietly complied to avoid unwanted attention? How many of us have sought to rank ourselves in comparison with our peers? How many have lost sight of a child in the pursuit of results? How many of us have changed our teaching to suit what we imagine an inspector is looking for? In all these ways, we collude in the system we say we deplore. This book argues for revolution, but this is not so simple an act as rising up and overthrowing an oppressor. We need to rise up against our own worst natures. We need to evolve in order to thrive, and so this form of evolution might be better conceptualised as (r)evolution. There will be uncomfortable home truths to be considered throughout, but in facing them we will put ourselves in a position worthy of trust and we will be ready to take control of our profession. There will be many who seek to stand in the way of genuine teacher autonomy so we may need to use weapons of mass construction. These weapons are rhizomatic – they connect at grassroots levels in creative

---

4 Michael Gove, I Refuse to Surrender to the Marxist Teachers Hell-Bent on Destroying Our Schools, *Daily Mail* (23 March 2013). Available at: http://www.dailymail.co.uk/debate/article-2298146/I-refuse-surrender-Marxist-teachers-hell-bent-destroying-schools-Education-Secretary-berates-new-enemies-promise-opposing-plans.html.

and unpredictable ways. They are weapons of hope. And they are in our hands, every day in the classroom.

This book aims to explore not only what these weapons are and how to use them but why they are needed. It examines what is happening in education across the world and how the hyperactive pace of change and narratives of failure are damaging children in order to protect the interests of a few individuals. It aims to expose what is, in my opinion, a system of child abuse so widespread and openly enacted that few can see it for what it is. What kind of future do we really want for our children and what kind of education would deliver it?

Chapter 1

DEAD MAN'S CLOTHING

Bruno took off his overcoat and placed it as gently as possible on the ground. Then he took off his shirt and shivered for a moment in the cold air before putting on the pyjama top. As it slipped over his head he made the mistake of breathing through his nose; it did not smell very nice.

'When was this last washed?' he called out and Shmuel turned around.

'I don't know if it's ever been washed,' said Shmuel.

John Boyne, *The Boy in the Striped Pyjamas* (2006)

In *The Boy in the Striped Pyjamas*, lonely Bruno, son of the Commandant, is desperate to join his new friend Shmuel on the other side of the fence. He thinks it will be fun. He has no idea that the other side is Auschwitz or that he is in danger. When Bruno dons his pyjamas and breathes in the odour of their previous occupant(s), he seals his fate. It is a moment of quite extraordinary complexity. It seems that in that whiff we get a compressed slice of time in which all possibilities are present and then closed down. The half-naked, shivering, innocent child stands there to be dressed in a future. Of all the clothes he could wear, he puts on the uniform of the concentration camp inmate. And there, in those clothes, are the past lives of the dead, the present life of Bruno and all his possible futures being narrowed into one awful outcome. It is a small detail packed with power. And one that constantly reminds me of our education system. That is a pretty contentious statement, I know. Perhaps I ought to explain.

Our entire education system is predicated on the appearance of order and uniformity. Perhaps this is most obviously evident in the assumption that children perform in neat, straight lines of progress, roughly in line with their chronological age. This presupposed trajectory is deemed so reliable that every teacher in the country is judged against it. Nowhere on this line is there room for sickness, bereavement, neglect or abuse. Nor is there room for difference, diversity of talent or aptitude. Young people are judged by their ability to keep marching on a straight and narrow pathway, resisting the temptation to follow an interest or question the status quo.

Within this system, examinations have always acted as a sorting hat to send children into their futures – handing out garments labelled A, B, C and so on – and marking out potential. It has always been a blunt and unforgiving tool and none of the numerous attempts to democratise it have ever really worked. There have been changes along the way – from the divisive O level/CSE split to GCSEs, towards the open sharing of criteria, the right to a re-mark and to see the original paper with annotations and comments (one exam board once sent papers back to us on which an examiner had written his comments in Ancient Greek in an attempt to avoid being read), resits, coursework and then back again – each change designed to keep the 'integrity' of the system intact without actually questioning the system. Febreze.

It seems that we nearly all accept that examinations are necessary, so what we usually argue about is whether or not they should be washed. I would argue that we need new clothes. This acceptance of examinations being the 'best' way to assess our children is as outdated as consulting the oracle, but we persist in the belief because to do anything different just feels too complicated. We ignore evidence that questions the wisdom of the system and blindly accept that which props it up. This is an irresponsible act of neglect. The disproportionately adverse effect of high stakes testing on children with special educational needs (SEN)[1] and those children from ethnic minorities[2] made a mockery of the notion of No Child Left Behind in the US and Every Child Matters in the UK. Although the slogans have disappeared, the idea of a one-size-fits-all approach to testing has been strengthened by successive governments and is rarely challenged. How often do we, as a profession, really consider the necessity of high stakes national examinations and the impact they have on our practice?

Consider:

- How much of your teaching time is dedicated to preparing for the demands of the exam?

- How much of your marking feedback focuses on the requirements of the exam?

- Have you ever said to an enthusiastic child, 'You don't need that for the exam'?

- Have you ever stopped teaching something you loved/valued because it was taken off the syllabus?

- Do you ever avoid teaching a significant news event because it won't be relevant to the exam?

----

1 Antonis Katsiyannis, Dalun Zhang, Joseph B. Ryan and Julie Jones, High-Stakes Testing and Students with Disabilities: Challenges and Promises, *Journal of Disability Policy Studies* 18(3) (2007): 160–167.

2 Sandra J. Altshuler and Tresa Schmautz, No Hispanic Student Left Behind: The Consequence of 'High Stakes' Testing, *Children and Schools: A Journal of the National Association of Social Workers* 28(1) (2005): 5–14.

♦ Do you ever find that the information on the syllabus is actually out of date because the exam can't keep pace with the theory or new ideas emerging from your specialist field?

Think about it. What if you were instead judged on:

♦ Whether or not pupils were well rounded and articulate.

♦ Whether they were happy at school and felt stimulated.

♦ Whether they were hopeful about their future.

♦ Whether they had the skills to be active participants in society.

♦ Whether they could spot deception, manipulation and bias in the media.

♦ Whether they were wise.

♦ Whether they were responsible for themselves and others.

♦ Whether they were kind.

♦ Whether they understood how to effect change in the world.

♦ Whether they remembered your lessons five years after they had left school.

How would this change our teaching? This is not an anti-knowledge list – being well rounded includes knowing stuff about the world. But what if we were judged on the long term, meaningful connection of that 'stuff' to our lives? What if it was an expectation that children would use, enjoy and retain what we teach? Not only would our pedagogy have to change but the whole basis on which we conduct our research would too. At this moment in time, the vast majority of educational research which claims to tell us 'what works' simply uses test performances as an indicator. It is a shamefully short sighted way to look at effectiveness in education.

High stakes testing not only shapes the questions we choose to ask in our research but also it shapes Ofsted judgements and therefore becomes the single most influential factor in the survival of a school. It affects perceptions of staff effectiveness and leads us to manipulate data to play the system. It segregates and cements a child's perception of self and others. It fails to acknowledge difference, difficulty, diversity and desire. And it survives for one reason: because the individuals who make the decisions did well out of that system, so why change it? Well, that's exactly why we *should* change it.

Outside of the classroom, there are strong voices all over the world questioning the wisdom of high stakes testing, and the drum is getting louder. In the US, Daniel Willingham, in his customary balanced way, insists that we need a real debate about the role of testing in schools,[3] while Pasi Sahlberg calls for an uncoupling of assessment and accountability structures,[4] elsewhere pointing to the importance of trust in ensuring high standards in education:

Shared responsibility has created strong mutual trust within [the] Finnish education system that [sic] is one frequently mentioned success factor of Finnish education. As a result, we

---

3   Daniel Willingham, How to Make Edu-Blogging Less Boring, *Daniel Willingham* (30 July 2013). Available at: http://www.danielwillingham.com/1/post/2013/07/how-to-make-edu-blogging-less-boring.html.

4   Pasi Sahlberg, Rethinking Accountability in a Knowledge Society, *Journal of Educational Change* 11 (2010): 45–61. Available at: http://pasisahlberg.com/wp-content/uploads/2013/01/Rethinking-accountability-JEC-2010.pdf.

don't need external standardized tests, teacher evaluation or inspection to assure high quality.[5]

As long ago as 1996, strong doubts were being raised about the reliability of testing, pointing to the discrepancies between the marking even from the *same* examiner[6] – a situation that has only worsened in recent years as exam boards have struggled to cope with multiple entries and schools have become more likely to demand re-marks. Couple these concerns with the interference of various governments and we see the fiascos that beset the GCSE examinations in the UK in 2010 and the SATs examinations in the US in 2009. John Wilmut and colleagues, in their assessment of the reliability of exams, suggest that essay-based examinations are more at risk of unreliable marking than short responses or multiple choice, yet the latter are seen as soft options. Dylan Wiliam's hinge questions show that intelligent short multiple choice questions can, in fact, reveal key misconceptions in children's learning and can provide high levels of thinking and reasoning.[7] It stands to reason that if tests are to be effective, they should focus on being checkpoints for the understanding of key foundation concepts; used as low stakes internal processes, not external

5 Pasi Sahlberg, Four Questions About Education in Finland, *Pasi Sahlberg Blog* (9 April 2012). Available at: http://pasisahlberg.com/four-questions-about-education-in-finland/.

6 John Wilmut, Robert Wood and Roger Murphy, A Review of Research into the Reliability of Examinations. Discussion paper prepared for the School Curriculum and Assessment Authority, University of Nottingham (1996). Available at: http://www.nottingham.ac.uk/education/centres/cdell/pdf-reportsrelexam/relexam.pdf.

7 Caroline Wylie and Dylan Wiliam, Analyzing Diagnostic Items: What Makes a Student Response Interpretable? Paper presented at the annual meeting of the National Council on Measurement in Education, Chicago, IL, April 2006. Available at: http://www.dylanwiliam.org/Dylan_Wiliams_website/Papers_files/DIMS%20%28NCME%202007%29.pdf.

end points. And they should not masquerade as an adequate and reliable means of assessing depth and criticality.

Structural skills, such as writing essays, may well be better assessed in ways other than through examination, but this would rely on building alternative assessment structures and beginning to trust teachers to manage those systems. Until assessment is uncoupled from accountability, and the grades of a child are disconnected from the pay and conditions of their teachers, such trust will be undermined by what some have termed as 'game play' and I prefer to call 'survival strategy'. Whatever the solution, it seems that everyone knows the system is in a mess but few want to clear it up.

As well as removing the high stakes element to examinations for teachers, we need to do the same for children. It may take more than one attempt to get through a checkpoint but the border should always remain open to further attempts. Turning children away from trying again slams a door in the face of their futures. It undermines the importance of resilience, persistence and grit. We need to be clear: graduating from school successfully should indicate that one has reached a certain standard. Whether it took several attempts to get there should be of little consequence; we allow people to take many driving tests because it is important to ensure that, once they have passed, they are safe. If we apply the same logic to education, we simply say that once they have passed, they are educated to a reasonable standard. Should certain universities or employers care whether or not the student was able to 'pass' first time, they can see this from their records. To give children one shot at success is an act of gross irresponsibility, both from a humanitarian and economic point of view. Where on earth is the sense in writing off a large section of the population, not because they couldn't but because they needed a little longer?

Already in the UK, the coalition government's decision to take only the first grade as the one that counts for school league tables is leading to some highly unethical practices in schools. For example, to protect the league tables in my son's school, all Year 10 GCSE science exams were cancelled and the decision taken to enter pupils for all units in Year 11. This meant that his grade A, already taken and awarded for his first unit, was discounted, as were other high grades, because *on the whole* it was felt that the year group might not do well if the first GCSE was submitted in Year 10. Unless you were a teacher, the letter that went out to parents was almost entirely incomprehensible, but it argued that the decision was in the best interests of pupils. In reality, it was in the sole interest of the school. The idea here, that the best way to judge the summative achievement of eleven years of education is by putting children through a series of highly pressured exams in the space of one month, is clearly insane. Why do we do it? Because that is how we used to do it? There seems to be no other explanation.

I am not making the case that all tests are bad, but assuming that everything that is worth learning can be tested in an examination is simply lazy. There *is* some compelling evidence in the field of cognitive psychology that regular low stakes testing can help to build secure knowledge content in the memory,[8] and certainly for those elements of knowledge schema on which more complex ideas are built, it is a useful tool. But, even so, much of this research only looks so far as to check whether the information tested in

---

8   John Dunlosky, Katherine Rawson, Elizabeth Marsh, Mitchell Nathan and
     Daniel Willingham, Improving Students' Learning with Effective Learning
     Techniques: Promising Directions from Cognitive and Education Psychology,
     Psychological Science in the Public Interest 14 (2013): 4–58.

low stakes tests was retained successfully for the high stakes test, not whether it was retained in the longer term. It seems that nobody has really thought to look *beyond* the exam. Surely, if we want children to leave school with information that stays with them for life, we should be scrutinising this more carefully.

As a species, our obsession with measuring and certainty has driven us to a point of near despair and to moments of blind acceptance of the shiny and new. John Hattie's effect sizes were hailed as an answer to the ubiquitous question, 'What works?'[9] How easy it seemed to be to scan down a list of interventions and see which ones were most effective,[10] but as Dylan Wiliam points out, effect sizes are highly flawed in assessing anything as complex as learning.[11] He explains that effect sizes may work in medicine where it is possible to ascertain whether or not a cure has worked, but for education it is very hard to prove correlation between a single factor/intervention and success in an exam. Indeed, the very nature of the test will yield different results. Not only are the methods of effect sizes flawed but those flaws expose weaknesses in test-to-test validity. In fact, in a lengthy and detailed analysis of different kinds of testing, he notes: 'Ruiz-Primo et al. (2002) found that the closer the assessment was to the enactment of the curriculum, the greater

---

9   John Hattie, *Visible Learning: A Synthesis of Over 800 Meta-Analyses Relating to Achievement* (London: Routledge, 2009).

10 Sutton Trust and Education Endowment Foundation, *Teaching and Learning Toolkit* (London: Education Endowment Foundation, 2013). Available at: http://educationendowmentfoundation.org.uk/uploads/toolkit/Teaching_and_Learning_Toolkit_%28Spring_2013%29.pdf.

11 Dylan Wiliam, An Integrative Summary of the Research Literature and Implications for a New Theory of Formative Assessment, in Heidi L. Andrade and Gregory J. Cizek (eds.), *Handbook of Formative Assessment* (New York and Abingdon: Routledge, 2010), pp. 18–40.

was the sensitivity of the assessment to the effects of instruction, and that the impact was considerable'.[12]

It stands to reason then that where effects are greatest there has been more alignment between the teaching and the test. Where assessments are proximal (i.e. related to content but indirectly) it is very difficult to prove that one intervention works above another. This creates huge difficulties for us as teachers. We can improve results but only in the knowledge that the result will probably not translate into learning which will be applied in more proximal contexts, such as further study or the workplace. We need to think carefully about the alignment of our teaching and assessment with long term goals.

It is a common complaint from teachers that, on starting a new course, children who move up with a number of good grades at SATs, GCSE or A level seem to be disappointingly below the level that their grade would suggest. Over the years, I've heard many frustrated teachers of Years 3, 7, 12 as well as undergraduates exclaim, 'There is no way he/she is a level 3/5/grade C/A', and throw their hands up in despair as they consider the implications of those levels on their own progress data. The simple fact is that if we tell children the knowledge they are learning is for an examination, then when the examination is over they will see no point in retaining it. Perhaps someone could research that? The dumping effect.

We know from neuroscience that the brain will prune out synaptic links that are underused or deemed unimportant.

12 Wiliam, An Integrative Summary of the Research Literature, p. 22, citing: Maria Ruiz-Primo, Richard J. Shavelson, Laura Hamilton and Steve Klein, On the Evaluation of Systemic Science Education Reform: Searching for Instructional Sensitivity, *Journal of Research in Science Teaching* 39(5) (2002): 369–393.

This 'neural Darwinism' is one of the significant strategies we have for coping with overload.[13] But how quickly does it happen and is there anything we can do to ensure that learning stays in the mind beyond the exam? What if:

♦ We only mentioned examinations in terms of an aside – something that will happen but which is not central to the importance of what is being learned?

♦ We went beyond the syllabus?

♦ We focused on what makes learning *really* memorable in the long term, that is emotion,[14] activity[15] and narrative?[16]

One not-very-Old Etonian gave me an image of what this world might be like when he said of his school experience:

The exams are something we know we will do, but there is an assumption that we'll do well – they're almost irrelevant. The focus is not on the exam, but on really engaging with and understanding what is being learned. And if you have an interest or talent, like you love drama or sport or something, school does everything it can to support you – you're encouraged to follow your passion. It's a great place.

13 Gerald M. Edelman, *The Mindful Brain: Cortical Organization and the Group-Selective Theory of Higher Brain Function* (Cambridge, MA: MIT Press, 1982).

14 Robert Sylwester, How Emotions Affect Learning, *Educational Leadership* 52(2) (1994): 60–65. Available at: http://www.ascd.org/publications/educational-leadership/oct94/vol52/num02/How-Emotions-Affect-Learning.aspx.

15 Claudia Erni Baumann and Roman Boutellier, Physical Activity: The Basis of Learning and Creativity. Paper presented at the Future of Education Conference, Florence, Italy, 7–8 June 2012. Available at: http://conference.pixel-online.net/edu_future/common/download/Paper_pdf/ITL59-Baumann.pdf.

16 Diana Arya and Andrew Maul, The Role of the Scientific Discovery Narrative in Middle School Science Education: An Experimental Study, *Journal of Educational Psychology* 104(4) (2012): 1022–1032.

How could we build an Eton ethos in every school? I know, of course, that not every school has the facilities or funding as that of Eton, but any school can build an ethos on the principle that learning is something to be loved *for its own sake*, and that when a child has a passion it is the duty of the education system to allow it to thrive (even if it falls out of the EBacc measure). That makes for memorable learning. They knew me. They encouraged me. They loved me and I learned.

It seems to me that a system designed to ensure quality is the very thing undermining quality. There is not even correlation between the different types of examination that a child might take at the same age. A child performing well in a GCSE in the UK or a SAT in the US may not perform well on an international PISA test – each examination system is testing different skills. Robert Coe's inaugural lecture on the comparisons between GCSEs and international tests drew the conclusion that there must have been grade inflation at GCSE over the last twenty years in order for the improvements in grades not to be reflected in international tests.[17] At the same time, Oxford University published research that challenged the notion of grade inflation.[18] What are we to think?

People tend to choose the research that best fits their world view. But there is another explanation that is simply about the limitations of tests. Examinations, like running, demand

---

17 Robert Coe, Improving Education: A Triumph of Hope Over Experience. Inaugural lecture, Centre for Evaluation and Monitoring, Durham University, 2013. Available at: http://www.cem.org/attachments/publications/ImprovingEducation2013.pdf.

18 Jo-Anne Baird, Ayesha Ahmed, Therese Hopfenbeck, Carol Brown and Victoria Elliot, Research Evidence Relating to Proposals for Reform of the GCSE. Oxford University Centre for Educational Assessment Report: OUCEA/13/1 (2013). Available at: http://oucea.education.ox.ac.uk/wordpress/wp-content/uploads/2013/04/WCQ-report-final.pdf.

different things. Some are sprints. Some contain hurdles. Some are marathons. You are not comparing like with like, so it is necessary to take considerable care when deciding how to assess children – for example, which applications of knowledge we need and how best to exploit them. This does not mean we should make our GCSEs more like PISA tests, but we should begin to recognise that there is a limitation to measuring children on examination performance. In my view, this leads to a devastating waste of human potential.

If you were designing an education system, would you model it on a call centre, with everyone reading from the same script, or on Apple or the Eden Project where creativity, passion, the generation of ideas and an acceptance of difference are deemed to be important elements of the working culture? In the words of Tim Smit, founder of the Eden Project:

If you love something and you are not a freak, there will be millions of other people who will also see the magic in what you love. If you find that thing, the only problem you will have is in finding a way to tell other people about it. Tell another person. ... Human beings must have hope.[19]

Where is the hope in our current assessment systems? Where are the dreams? A genuinely inclusive education system would facilitate the building of dreams. Instead, we have become complicit in the act of dream slaying.

Politicians speak of business. They claim that they are creating education systems to ensure that businesses thrive in the future but they ignore the reality. Leaping straight from an

19 Tim Smit, address to schoolchildren at the ISTA Eden Project Middle School Festival, February 2014.

Oxbridge degree into politics, an advisory position or a think-tank means that few of those affecting policy really understand how businesses work or how any of the institutions they are entrusted to run operate.[20] Degrees in History or English do not adequately prepare people, no matter how intelligent, for highly complex offices of responsibility in finance, health or education. In what other profession would a lack of experience and relevant knowledge be so readily accepted? The point is an important one, for it underlines the idea that an academic education in any subject offers sufficient grounding to make decisions that affect the lives of an entire population. Instead, either we need to have a political class drawn from the fields they represent or we need to give more professional autonomy to those working in fields such as education, allowing them to run their own affairs for the long term. This assumption that academic = competent is a problem for our young too, because it automatically undermines the validity of vocational qualifications. It is interesting, for example, that media studies is so universally derided by those who entered and work in the media without studying the subject.

Where business does impact on education, however, is in the realm of profit making, and, when we take a closer look at this, we see a strong vested interest in maintaining the role of examinations and testing and in promoting the use of textbooks and pre-packaged curriculum materials. One example is the much quoted and pervasive influence of the Pearson Education group. Pearson, as the leading publisher of education textbooks, stand to profit from Conservative policy to promote the use of textbooks in the classroom and

---

20 Fiona Millar, Who Is Really Behind Michael Gove's Big Education Ideas?, *The Guardian* (3 December 2013). Available at: http://www.theguardian.com/education/2013/dec/03/michael-gove-education-dominic-cummings-policies-oxbridge.

they are already trialling a pre-packaged curriculum loaded tablet in six secondary schools in the UK.[21] They are closely aligned to TeachFirst, so have influence on teacher training. They own Edexcel and have the contract to set and mark SATs papers. In effect, they are the most influential operator of assessment. In addition, Pearson have set up a think-tank to influence policy, responding to government calls for 'evidence-based practice'. Whatever the intentions behind this – and I do not doubt the integrity of some of the academics who have conducted Pearson funded research – I do have concerns. For one company to have so much influence over curriculum materials, assessment, teacher training routes and educational research is, in my opinion, dangerous. Even if the motivations are altruistic and not materialistic, a monopoly of this size, geared to making profit, cannot be in the best interests of children and can only stifle proper debate. Are Pearson going to commission research into an alternative to examinations? Probably not.

Elsewhere in the business world, the Confederation of British Industry (CBI) have repeatedly called for more practical application of skills in schools, particularly in science and design technology.[22] They have petitioned for more work experience, more creativity and, yes, firmer foundations in literacy and numeracy. Literacy and numeracy are the lowest common denominators we should be aiming for.

----

21 Elizabeth Truss, Elizabeth Truss Speaks About Improving Teaching. Speech delivered at Reform, London, 10 April 2014. Available at: https://www.gov.uk/government/speeches/elizabeth-truss-speaks-about-improving-teaching.

22 Richard Garner, 'Sheer Scale of Prescription' Under Michael Gove's Planned New Curriculum Will Turn Pupils Off Science Lessons, Warn Business Leaders, *The Independent* (16 April 2013). Available at: http://www.independent.co.uk/news/business/news/sheer-scale-of-prescription-under-michael-goves-planned-new-curriculum-will-turn-pupils-off-science-lessons-warn-business-leaders-8575614.html.

They are an entitlement. But children need more than that to thrive.

If we were really business minded we would value the arts. Not only do the creative industries now employ more people than construction but creative thinking is key in all areas of working life. Yet the take up of arts subjects has fallen dramatically since the EBacc was introduced and the significant work of initiatives such as Creative Partnerships under the Labour government of 1997–2010 were unceremoniously dumped by the incoming cabinet. Similarly, if we were business minded, we would put work experience into the curriculum as a right of every child. We would invest in high quality careers advice – the 2013 Select Committee Report on this area of education was damning:

Independent careers advice and guidance has never been as important for young people as it is today. Too many schools lack the skills, incentives or capacity to fulfil the duty put upon them without a number of changes being made. Young people deserve better than the service they are likely to receive under the current arrangements. Schools cannot simply be left to get on with it.[23]

We would make evident to children all the varied pathways that exist in life and value the diversity of their talents. We would not seek to homogenise and, in appreciating and nurturing diversity, we would start to build assessment systems that allowed for a range of talents to be nurtured. The work of the Headteachers' Roundtable and their proposals for a

23 House of Commons Education Committee, *Careers Guidance for Young People: The Impact of the New Duty on Schools. Seventh Report of Session 2012–13.* Ref: HC 632-I (London: The Stationery Office Limited). Available at: http://www. publications.parliament.uk/pa/cm201213/cmselect/cmeduc/632/632.pdf, p. 4.

Baccalaureate (a real one, not an 'all my favourite subjects' one) is very promising[24] – it offers a stepping stone to a more balanced and egalitarian future.

Of course, the biggest barrier to the kinds of changes to assessment that would revolutionise our education system is the endemic lack of trust in teachers across many countries. No significant, meaningful change will occur unless this trust is built – something I will consider in future chapters. But it seems, right now, that this lack of trust, combined with an obsession with measuring, is rooted in fear. A fear of the future.

----

24 Headteachers' Roundtable, Qualifications Framework Proposal (May 2013). Available at: http://headteachersroundtable.files.wordpress.com/2013/05/the-headteachers-roundtable-qualifications-framework-proposal-final.pdf.

Chapter 2

THE FUTURE: RUN OR RIDE?

If we open up a quarrel between the past and the present, we shall find that we have lost the future.

**Winston Churchill,
address to the House of Commons (18 June 1940)**

When Churchill issued this warning to the House of Commons in 1940, there was a clear, present and immediate danger, so it may seem crass to evoke these words now. But just because danger is not clearly present, it does not mean that it has no immediacy. Our world is changing so quickly, so *presently* and so radically that our future is simultaneously becoming our past even as we dither. When our global monetary systems are operating at nano-speeds of 126 millionths of a second,[1] even the words 'blink and you've missed it' are too slow. As we teachers and politicians argue about whether or not the Glorious Revolution or Dickens should be at the heart of the curriculum, civilisation is changing at a pace that has never before occurred in the history of mankind. This is creating an enormous divide in the world of education between those who think we build better futures by linking to the past and those who argue that a

---

1   Robert Charette, London Stock Exchange New Trading Platform 'Twice as Fast' as Rivals, *IEEE Spectrum* (20 October 2010). Available at: http:// spectrum.ieee.org/riskfactor/computing/it/london-stock-exchange-new-trading-platform-twice-as-fast-as-rivals.

constructive future requires leaving the past behind us. We can continue to tinker and consider, playing, as Newton said, with pebbles on the beach or we can get into the water. The ocean is coming at us. The question is, do we run away or ride the wave? In this chapter, I will look at how the concept of future has become laden with guilt and functions as a control mechanism – what the philosopher Gilles Deleuze would call the 'modulating cast of a control society'.[2]

Deleuze conceptualises time as a complex and multi-faceted concept,[3] which is not linear in the way we like to think of it. He divides time into *now* time (chronos) – being in the present moment, in a smooth space of possibility and absorption – and *other* time (aion) – where shoots from the past and all possible futures snag on the present, forming new lines of action and reforming and reinterpreting old ones. It is aion time that interrupts learning and simultaneously offers possibilities as well as problems. It is one of the reasons that we can never truly predict outcomes – as any teacher who has ever had a wasp enter the room can tell you!

We assume in education that time, like progress, is linear, but it is not. We have all had hours that drag and hours that fly. Time is always experienced relatively, so we need to be aiming to help children to think differently about the ways in which time is presented to and experienced by them. This is far more important than we think. Cognitive scientist George Lakoff's moral frames theory suggests that the way we construct morality in our minds is dependent on the

---

2 Gilles Deleuze, Postscript on the Control Societies, *October* 59 (Winter 1992): 3–7.

3 Gilles Deleuze, *The Logic of Sense*, tr. Mark Lester with Charles Stivale, ed. Constantin V. Boundas (New York: Colombia University Press, 1990 [1969]).

frames and values built throughout childhood.[4] These will shape the way we view reality. It is not, he states, good enough to see people as 'good' or 'bad'. Instead, we need to accept that the constructs of morality are largely unconscious, have been built over time and shape the way we reason and justify our decisions. As teachers, we carry great responsibility in shaping the frames within which children will conceptualise the world and their place in it. We, their parents, communities and friends, are instrumental in building young people's future perceptions of reality. So, let's not reduce the English language GCSE course to an analysis of gossip magazines or history to a series of dates. Let's use the present to build narratives of hope for the future.

The future of education

One of the problems with the future is that, as Al Gore points out, most of us lack the imagination to see it as anything other than like the present but with better technology.[5] Yet one downside of technology is that it has brought with it a sense that our present is somehow less satisfactory than the past – perhaps this is based on our access to news and the general rule of thumb that good news is no news. We struggle to imagine the future. We mistrust our present. We romanticise our past, which is always positioned in complex relation to our emotions and experiences. Our tendency to think about past, present and future in these ways makes us

---

4 See Zoe Williams, George Lakoff: 'Conservatives Don't Follow the Polls, They Want to Change Them ... Liberals Do Everything Wrong', *The Guardian*, 1 February 2014. Available at: http://www.theguardian.com/books/2014/feb/01/george-lakoff-interview.

5 Al Gore, *Future: Six Drivers of Global Change* (New York: Random House, 2013).

prone to impose on education either the same experience that we had (if it was good) or the opposite (if it was bad). We rarely think to offer the completely new. What's worse, in order to control children, we constantly bombard them with a belief that the future is more important than the present and that they are doomed if they don't prepare for it. However, we rarely prepare ourselves or them for what that future might require – and I mean the future waiting for them beyond the test. Instead, we teachers react like pinballs to whatever present initiative we are assailed with, moving from specious present to specious present, from observation and Ofsted to observation without an eye on any date beyond that of the next results day.

To really understand the ways in which we have ignored the realities of time, we would have to move between philosophy and science in a way that is perhaps beyond the remit of this book. However, in both disciplines the differences between time as a measured entity and one that is experienced are significant. From quantum leaps to complexity theory, science itself is engrossed in the complexities of time in a way that education wilfully ignores.[6] Yet, the ways in which humans experience time offer some really interesting possibilities for reconceptualising classroom practice and our expectations of children and progress.

As a species, we want certainty and what better way of being certain than to attempt to ensure that our future looks like the best aspects of our past. We think we are marching forwards, but we are looped in longing for that which is gone. Attempting to make this loop look like a line is getting us into all kinds of trouble.

----

6   James Williams, *Gilles Deleuze's Philosophy of Time: A Critical Introduction and Guide* (Edinburgh: Edinburgh University Press, 2011).

For governments, and society as a whole, part of the problem is that we have not yet come to terms with the idea that full employment might be a thing of the past. My parents' generation, moving into work in the 1960s, describe a job market in which you could walk out of one job in the morning if you didn't like it and into another in the afternoon. School was not so much a place that prepared you for whether or not you might be employed but more for the kind of employment that you might expect. Schools were a holding pen to sort out those who would labour and those who would lead. We now attempt to offer a more egalitarian promise of hard work = good job. We dangle this carrot in front of children's noses, and for those who are raised in areas where employment is a given it may work. But for those who live in communities blighted by unemployment it is much more difficult. Equating education with future employment might be a goal for society, but for children? We might as well try to tempt them with broccoli.

However successfully we educate our young, we will never be able to provide the quantity of highly paid jobs that we have promised. Indeed, we will always need people to serve our food, clean our streets and care for our elderly. Let's assume that the socialist ideal that all citizens are equally valued and rewarded for their work is not coming to our shores any time soon. What then? How do we prepare children for the fact that they may never be employed or highly paid, even if they try hard? It is an idea so painful to focus on that it is no wonder we prefer to push our eyes into the sand. But if we blink and take a sideways look at the purpose of education we can find solutions, both economically and educationally.

There is an idea circulating among economists that one answer might lie in paying people 'to be alive'.[7] The policy, known as 'the basic income movement' and conceived by an artist rather than an economist, is that if all people were paid a basic living income by the government, regardless of wealth, poverty would disappear. On the surface, it seems like madness – a welfare state gone crazy – but some economists are seriously considering the proposal. Poverty impacts on education and health spending, housing, crime and a myriad of other areas. Eradicating it might well save governments more money than they would have to spend on basic income. But there might be other benefits too. People might be able to afford to stay at home with their children, care for elderly parents, work fewer hours, thereby reducing stress related illness, and contribute time to community and charity projects.

In fact, the idea is so appealing that it is uniting both left and right in the US in a serious consideration of the idea. The economist Evelyn Forget has researched an early pilot of the idea in Canada. She analysed the figures and concluded that were the US government to recreate the experiment on a national level by giving every citizen in the country $10,000 per year, poverty would be eradicated.[8] Indeed, not only do the figures make economic sense but there were other side effects – for example, school graduation rates increased and hospitalisation rates decreased. Basic minimum income economic policy might work, but it would need to work in partnership with education. It

---

7   Annie Lowrey, Switzerland's Proposal to Pay People for Being Alive, *New York Times* (12 November 2013). Available at: http://mobile.nytimes.com/2013/11/17/magazine/switzerlands-proposal-to-pay-people-for-being-alive.html.

8   Interview with Evelyn Forget, *Basic Income UK* (7 August 2013). Available at: www.basicincome.org.uk/interview/2013/08/health-forget-mincome-poverty/.

would shift the goals of education away from future economic survival, but towards what?

How might education be received by children if the long term promise was not employment but a fulfilling life? And if that promise was not held as a long term goal but started now – our fulfilling life started in the here and now? What if our society accepted that while not everyone might be able to earn, they still might love to learn? What if the goal was to be wise? In his book, *Authentic Happiness*, Martin Seligman refers to Aristotle's notion of 'eudaimonia', a good life – a life given gratification through the attempt to live with noble purpose.[9] What might an education with that aim look like? It would be more hopeful for a start and studies show us that having a sense of optimism about the future is crucial to our long term happiness.[10] It seems to me that, instead of hope and happiness, we build an image for our children of a future to be feared (unless you do as I say). We wrap it up, of course. We wrap it in a lie.

Trying to convince children that hard work will lead to economic success is futile. They only have to switch on the news to hear the lie exposed. They see instant celebrity through reality television shows, such as *The X Factor*, which perpetuate the myth that talent is innate. They are fed lines about millionaires with no qualifications, such as Lord Sugar or Richard Branson, neatly ignoring the hard work, determination and good luck that have led to these few successes. They learn that kicking a football into a net is worth more than saving a life every time they read a headline about a footballer's salary. They hear that politicians are entitled to pay rises (11% was the recommendation for MPs

9 Martin Seligman, *Authentic Happiness: Using the New Positive Psychology to Realise Your Potential for Lasting Fulfilment* (New York: Free Press, 2002).

10 Martin Seligman, *Learned Optimism: How to Change Your Mind and Your Life* (New York: Knopf, 1991).

in 2013) while their own parents are laid off. These conflict-
ing signals create a great deal of confusion for children.
Poverty figures in the UK and US now show that the vast
majority of children living below the poverty line are in
working families[11] – the hard-working poor. They want to
believe the lie but they can't. That's not to say that we want
children to reject education – of course not. And, certainly,
getting qualifications gives them a better chance of economic success than not getting them. But we need to build
another vision of the future for children, one in which education has a purpose that reaches beyond employment.
How would this impact on the voluntary sector? How
would it impact on mental health? How would it impact on
crime? We need to think differently about time, and particularly about how we frame the concept of time for children.

Invariably, the vision of the future we present to children is
tainted with the past. We tell them that we wish we had
done things differently, imposing responsibility for our past
failures on them. We do this as teachers and as parents. As
governments, we tell them that previous governments have
failed and that they must put right this past failure. We tell
them that in the past Britain was great but now it is not and
that it is their responsibility to make our nation great again.
We feed them a series of narratives: we tell children that
they will need exams for the future, skills for the future, that
they will need to fight for survival in the face of competition
from pesky foreigners in the future and that the planet will
be falling apart in the future. The future of our country
depends on you. The future pensions of your parents
depend on you. The incontinence pads of an ageing
generation will need to be changed by you (unless you go to

----

11 Susan Heavey, Number of Working Poor Families Grows As Wealth Gap
    Widens, *Reuters* (15 January 2013). Available at: http://www.reuters.com/
    article/2013/01/15/us-usa-economy-workingpoor-idUSBRE90E05520130115.

a Russell Group university). No wonder our kids retreat into computer games and virtual worlds. They are retreating from the aionic slings and arrows of an imagined outrageous fortune. Teaching for wisdom and happiness is one way of mitigating this harm. And, be in no doubt, we are currently inflicting harm on our young.

We have conceptualised children as units of productivity almost from the moment they are born. From baseline testing in the Early Years, progressing up to P levels, phonics tests, SATs, grammar tests, progress grades, GCSEs, A levels, key skills, NVQs … they are little units moving through the production line in order to survive so that they can contribute to the economy, which as we know all too well, can't in itself be predicted. All of this combines into an almost blind moral panic about education in which the very concept of childhood is lost. For example, there was the bizarre response from Michael Gove to the Too Much, Too Soon campaign led by Sir Al Aynsley-Green (which argues for the rights of children to a safe and playful childhood)[12] that the government had a responsibility to ensure that 5-year-olds were being prepared to solve 'hard calculus'. The world has gone mad when childhood, happiness and play are considered to be threats to the nation. And this is not just a British problem: in the US, the pressure for children to be 'college ready' led to one school cancelling the annual kindergarten production in order to spend more time preparing children for tests.[13] In what view of childhood is that acceptable? Our narratives have moved beyond the romanticism of the 'misspent youth', in which it seemed acceptable to have a

---

12 See http://www.toomuchtoosoon.org/about.html.

13 Valerie Strauss, Kindergarten Show Canceled So Kids Can Keep Studying to Become 'College and Career Ready.' Really. *Washington Post* (26 April 2014). Available at: http://www.washingtonpost.com/blogs/answer-sheet/wp/2014/04/26/kindergarten-show-canceled-so-kids-can-keep-working-to-become-college-and-career-ready-really/.

period of experimentation and uncertainty in late adolescence, towards a torrent of terror that even babyhood might be wasted. The expectations we are piling onto our young are more indicative of adult neurosis than they are a reflection of the reality of the world we live in.

We know from thinkers like Charles Leadbeater and former US Vice President Al Gore that whatever the future holds, it will demand innovation. We know that there will be challenges. But human beings are creative and adaptable beings, and for every problem there will be a potential solution. The future is not a problem, it is an opportunity. And in the words of the old aphorism, the present is a gift.

We can combine the needs of the future and present by very simply giving children an education that they love *now*, in which they thrive *now*, in which they learn to love knowledge and learning because it's just really interesting and in which they become happy, articulate, resilient, agentive people with the capacity to embrace whatever future they eventually inhabit. This, according to Deleuze, is 'nomadic teaching' – teaching in response to the classroom landscape of interactions; a 'smooth space' in which all possibilities are present.[14] This takes place in chronos time, when possibility, thinking, hope and flow are possible. For example, I am with Year 5. We have 'discovered' a skeleton in a Tudor priest hole. There is no lying in this space – they know they are in school and not in a Tudor mansion, but in smooth space they suspend disbelief. All that matters is this moment: who is he and why is he here? They examine the artefacts around the body. They decode his warning letter. They learn about the past, the Reformation, by being absolutely present in the

---

14 Kaustuv Roy, *Teachers in Nomadic Spaces: Deleuze and Curriculum* (New York: Peter Lang, 2003). Available at: http://2020research.files.wordpress. com/2011/06/roy-deleuze-teachers-in-nomadic-spaces.pdf.

moment, in chronos. I guard them from aion – it is not right to point out that this information might be useful for an exam. They need to be fully immersed in this learning in order for it to matter. And it does. If we were to radically improve a child's experience of education in just three words, it would be this: make it matter.

Having your cake *and* eating it (which is what cakes were made for, after all)

The things we desire – wisdom, happiness, love of learning, self and others – are the vehicles from which we can access the essentials that we hear are needed from politicians and business leaders. We don't have to choose between skills and knowledge, between creativity and rigour. We can have both. But we need to be smarter. We are carried along in currents of accountability and assessment that have created the appearance of robustness. But when you squeeze out the tests and the time spent preparing for the tests, what are you left with? How might we view the passage of time differently?

Reconceptualising future

♦ Prepare children for the future by making the present more appealing.

♦ Make children believe they have something to offer the future by not only telling them all the stuff we already know but pointing out all that is yet to be discovered (by them).

♦ Never avoid the news – bring new events and ideas into your teaching as they happen, responding to present events and predicting future outcomes.

♦ Help them to understand how their brains work and why we are doing what we do (and the reason is never 'it will come in handy for the exam'). Teach them about plasticity in the brain and how their future potential is being created now.

♦ Teach them all kinds of knowledge but always framed within the question, 'Who in the world needs to know this stuff and why?', thereby opening up an understanding of the variety of the world of work and, with it, possible future pathways.

♦ Teach them to be in it for the long haul but that deep learning has periods of frustration. Do this by tapping into examples they will understand – the time it took them to master swimming/bike riding/keepy-uppy/ applying make-up effectively/living with a brace/learning to play an instrument. All children have overcome difficulties in learning, even if they don't remember. Remind them of the miracle of speaking, walking, using the toilet ...

♦ Teach them about happiness and human psychology, building an understanding that success is about more than money.

♦ Help them to build an image of a future in which work may not be the ultimate goal, but merely a means to funding a more fulfilling life. Let them explore that this life might contain sport, art and cultural visits, charity work, community projects and family time. Let them see that happy and fulfilling futures are possible separate from work, so that we remove the stigma from certain jobs and roles. You are not a loser if you end up working in Morrisons. Is that anti-aspirational or hopeful?

Reconceptualising present

♦ Introduce children to all the nowness of the world – what is currently happening in local, regional, national and global settings – and how these things affect them now.

♦ Show children that they can affect their learning now by reflecting on what they are doing and taking present actions.

♦ Show children that learning for learning's sake is rewarding by making it memorable and tangible. Show them that even rudimentary and seemingly dull tasks, like learning times tables and grammar, can be enlivened through multisensory activities, and that knowledge can be made more memorable through narratives and stories.

♦ Prove that you care as much about their now selves as you do about their future selves by showing them that you like them and by listening to them.

♦ Respond to the now by suspending what you planned if something arises. This might be an interesting question from a child. It might be a potential distraction or disruption. Reframe. If it starts to snow or a wasp enters the room, where is the potential learning now? How do we turn distractions into opportunities?

♦ Save time now by making connections between subjects. Where is the science in Ancient Egypt? The maths in

Ancient Greece? Remind staff that literacy and numeracy are not English and maths and that all subjects have a responsibility to attend to these vital skills (when and where relevant).

♦ Build in opportunities for children to make a difference to the world now through community projects, participation in political events, serving on school and local councils, voluntary work and work experience – many aspects of which have disappeared from school timetables in response to narrow accountability focuses.

Reconceptualising past

♦ Decide as professional adults which aspects of 'all the best that has been said and done' you are going to introduce into your curriculum. There isn't room for it all.

♦ Look for narratives of hope from the past – stories of survival and overcoming adversity in order to build a belief in human agency and endurance in young people.

♦ Always ask how the past has impacted on us in the present so that children see the past as connected to them.

♦ Link past events to their own family histories and local history. What was happening here when Athens was building a democracy? What effect did the First World War have on this town, on your family?

♦ Build a bank of success narratives drawn from ordinary as well as privileged lives. Celebrate local heroes like foster carers and volunteers. Bring those people into the school.

♦ Get children to use information from the past to make predictions about the future.

In short, we need to be taking a long view of learning, using time as a means to connect the dots – not necessarily in linear ways but in modes of resonance. In such ways we build connections in the minds of children. We train them to see patterns and possibilities. We become nomadic. We build hope. And to be working in the hope construction industry we have to be in it for a long period of time. Teaching is not a lily pad stop on the way to a better place.

Chapter 3

NEO-NARCISSISM: THE PROBLEM WITH INTERNATIONAL COMPARISONS

Is it not rather what we expect in men, that they should have numerous strands of experience lying side by side and never compare them with each other?

George Eliot, *Middlemarch* (1871–72)

When I was 7, my dad came home from a parents' evening. He sat me down and told me the news.

'Your teacher said that in the tests, out of a class of 31, you were number 30.'

I was very happy – 30 was a big number. Okay, so it wasn't quite as big as 31, but you have to have something to aim for, don't you? Thankfully, in those days, we didn't have progress charts or for the rest of my school days, based on that baseline data, I would have happily met my 'grades to beat' while woefully underperforming. But I digress.

I am sometimes reminded of my mathematical misconception when I listen to the government and media attempting to decipher the latest Organisation for Economic Co-operation and Development (OECD) statistics or examination results. Whatever the underlying message beneath the headline numbers, however complex it might be, the overriding narrative is always one of failure. And it is a narrative with widely damaging consequences because the failure is always connected to a thinly veiled fear of all that is foreign or different to 'us'. We cannot be happy that living standards are rising in line with educational achievements across the world. Instead we must be afraid. But what do the statistics really tell us? What can be learned?

Well, firstly, we see a woeful misunderstanding of the basic principles of numeracy that drive our accountability processes. Take, for example, this exchange between the Education Select Committee and the then Secretary of State for Education, Michael Gove, in 2013:

Q98 Chair: *… if 'good' requires pupil performance to exceed the national average, and if all schools must be good, how is this mathematically possible?*

Michael Gove: *By getting better all the time.*

Q99 Chair: *So it is possible, is it?*

Michael Gove: *It is possible to get better all the time.*

Q100 Chair: *Were you better at literacy than numeracy, Secretary of State?*

Michael Gove: *I cannot remember.[1]*

It may seem like a cheap shot to air blunders in this way, but the point is a serious one. We are told that standards of

---

1   Education Select Committee, The Responsibilities of the Secretary of State for Education, HC 1786-i, 2010–2012 (31 January 2012). Available at: http:// www.publications.parliament.uk/pa/cm201012/cmselect/cmeduc/uc1786-i/ uc178601.htm.

numerical understanding in this country are too low by people who themselves don't understand the numerical information they are using to make their claims. Even worse, too often the general public in many countries are manipulated into a way of thinking by a misuse of statistics simply in order to ease the passage of policy that does nothing to address the underlying problems beneath the data.

The data that most people use to judge whether or not we hold our own in the field of education comes from international comparison tests called PISA or TIMMS. In a nutshell, the difference between the two is that the first tests for the innovative application of knowledge and the second for a more basic assessment of knowledge. The fact that we tend to perform better in TIMMS than in PISA would suggest that it is not knowledge per se that is problematic for us, but rather the innovative application of it. Yet, in another PISA test (the more practical application of knowledge through problem solving), results released in 2014 showed English children (Scotland, Wales and Northern Ireland did not enter) performing highly.[2] This achievement was not mentioned positively once by the British government, presumably because it did not fit the dominant failure narrative. Instead, they focus on the impression that we are woefully behind our international competitors. There is a belief that there is a correlation between the PISA test and future gross domestic product,[3] but there is little consideration of other factors. For example, we know that the countries that perform best on PISA in the Western world are those with the lowest

---

2   Sean Coughlan, England's Schools Succeed in Problem-Solving Test, *BBC News* (1 April 2014). Available at: http://www.bbc.co.uk/news/education-26823184.

3   Eric Hanushek and Ludger Woessmann, *The High Cost of Low Educational Performance: The Long-Run Economic Impact of Improving PISA Outcomes* (Paris: OECD Programme for International Student Assessment, 2010). Available at: http://www.oecd.org/pisa/44417824.pdf.

levels of social inequality. On the basis of the economic correlation argument, Finland would be the richest nation on earth, but it is not. In the East, the places that score highest on PISA have educational expectations that children and parents will commit to long hours of private tuition. So, the picture is much more complex than high test score = economic output.

Time and again, our standing in the international comparison tests is offered as a justification for a type of education system that focuses relentlessly on the acquisition of knowledge alone. However, this focus will not impact on PISA scores which the OECD states are designed to test 'knowledge in real life situations'. Nothing the current coalition government has done in its entire term of office has helped children to *apply* knowledge in anything like a real life situation (instead children are inundated with nonsense words for the phonics test), while advances that had been made in this area under the previous government have been stripped back. References to skills have largely been removed from the national curriculum (one Department for Education insider told me, ' "Skills" is a banned word in the department – it is more acceptable to swear'). In primary school geography, for example, it is no longer a requirement that children should 'weigh evidence' or 'think independently'. Thinking has been replaced by the simple learning of facts. The antithesis of PISA philosophy. To use our demise down the PISA tables as a justification for such policy shifts is at best ignorant; at worst it is wilfully negligent. Furthermore, have we really fallen at all?

Ignoring our good performance in the separate problem solving test, the claim is that we have fallen in the main knowledge tests. The 2000 PISA tests showed the UK performing well – seventh for literacy, eighth for maths, fourth for science. By 2012, the position had 'dropped' to twenty-third, twenty-sixth and twenty-first respectively. Clearly my 7-year-old self would hail this as a triumph, but to everyone else it sounds bad. Until you consider:

♦ The OECD analysis itself identified the 2000 tests as flawed. The UK did not field a statistically strong sample and the international field was small. We may not have been as good as we thought we were.

♦ But let's pretend we were (Rule Britannia!). The results in 2009 and 2012 showed that the differences in scores between countries was so slight that the rankings hid a reality of difference that was 'statistically insignificant'. There were also many more countries taking part and many of them were crowded in similarity. We were more or less the same as many others. If we look at it in another way, it's like having a photo finish in the 100 metres – there may well be a winner but the difference between the two is trifling. This difficulty was also a trait of the 2013 adult literacy and numeracy tests which also suggested a 'woeful' performance.

♦ Many of the 'countries' at the top were actually states or cities – a little like the UK only entering for the tests kids from independent schools in Surrey. Shanghai, for example, near the top, is one of the richest cities in China and they won't enter their migrant (most deprived) population for the tests.

♦ What is clear is that countries that have used PISA to justify the marketisation of education through GERM (Global Education Reform Movement), common in the UK and US for example, fare worse than countries focusing on ensuring consistency of provision. GERM reform is characterised by market driven policies that attempt to apply capitalist principles of free choice of provision to public services. If anything is clear from the PISA data, as Pasi Sahlberg points out, it is that this policy has failed.[4]

Even so, it is always tempting to look at those who are performing consistently well at the top and to try to come to some conclusions about what it is they do. In fact, this is one of the reasons the OECD do the PISA tests at all – not to name and shame but to look at the common elements of successful systems.

One of the most successful countries, and most consistently successful over time, despite falling out of the top ten in 2012, is Finland. Although Finland has 'fallen', taken over by city states and countries from the East, it remains one of the highest performing Western systems. Let's assume, for a moment, that we don't want our children in school until 11 p.m. as they do in South Korea, or to mirror their teenage suicide rates, it is worth continuing to explore what it is that Finland specifically does so well. Indeed, since the mid-2000s governments from all over the world have flown in and out of Finland in order to understand the Finnish phenomenon. Unfortunately, their findings are often cherry-picked and badly implemented. Labour came back with the answer that master's degrees were the solution. They consequently funded a programme of free master's courses onto which thousands of teachers enthusiastically enrolled. This idea was dropped by the incoming Conservative government, creating a profession who were partly qualified to master's level. Next we'll get Master Teachers, we hear. But with no master's. And some of them might be girls.

---

4 Pasi Sahlberg, The PISA 2012 Scores Show the Failure of 'Market Based' Education Reform, *The Guardian* (8 December 2013). Available at: http://www.theguardian.com/commentisfree/2013/dec/08/pisa-education-test-scores-meaning.

The Conservatives decided not to bother learning from Finland at all and zoomed across to China and Singapore instead. There they found that children worked hard, teachers were highly valued with fewer contact hours and parents valued education so much that they spent thousands on private tuition (negating the impact of the state funded education system), but also that the governments there were actually looking to the UK to be more creative. Singapore's Teach Less, Learn More policy was almost entirely ignored by the government. Instead, they have decided to bring over some Chinese teachers to teach maths. That'll do the trick. And so, while shouting about PISA successes in the East, the government actually implemented market driven policies from the US, one of the few Western nations in the recent adult tests of literacy and numeracy which came below us. Don't bother trying to work out the logic – there isn't any. But there is a very bad smell.

Let's look a little more closely at this UK/US relationship. It seems that neither is happy with its own or each other's educational performance. So why are our policies mirroring one another so closely (and have done for some time – for example, No Child Left Behind/Every Child Matters). What is really at work here? Susan Robertson, of Bristol University, categorises the neo-liberal market forces influencing education policy in the GERM countries as a 'class project with three key aims: the (i) redistribution of wealth upward to the ruling elites through new structures of governance; (ii) transformation of education systems so that the production of workers for the economy is the primary mandate; and (iii) breaking down of education as a public sector monopoly, opening it up to strategic investment by for profit firms'.[5]

I can see many of the teachers I know losing interest at this point – 'I'm just not interested in politics.' But you should be, because this agenda influences every area of your working life. For a start, Robertson points out that in order for these aims to be achieved, the government must 'break down the institutionalised interests of teachers, teacher unions and those fractions of civil society who have supported the idea of education as a public good'.[6] What else is education for if not for public good? Well, let's look further.

What if education actually feeds a mentality of consumption that threatens the planet? What if education convinces children that the most important thing in life is to make and spend money? What if education seeks simply to encourage children to comply unquestioningly with commands? How would these goals be met? Through a blind focus on examination results and a 'good job'? Through the refocusing of childhood from play and activity towards compliance and stillness? Through the encouragement of rote learning and predefined programmes of core knowledge? Through the creation of pre-packaged tablets with curriculum materials and pedagogy handy for use (hello Pearson, hello Rupert Murdoch). What if whole academy chains were run by Tory donors sympathetic to and likely to benefit from a neo-liberal model? What if a new 'alternative' to a union was offered to teachers called Edapt, working in line with government principles? What if teacher training was largely

----

5   Susan L. Robertson, 'Remaking the World': Neo-Liberalism and the Transformation of Education and Teachers' Labour (Bristol: Centre for Globalisation, Education and Societies, University of Bristol, 2008). Available at: http://www.bris.ac.uk/education/people/academicStaff/edslr/publications/17slr, p. 2.

6   Robertson, 'Remaking the World', p. 2.

removed from the troublesome universities who question the status quo?

Who would complain? You would think that teachers and parents would, and so their attention must be diverted. I imagine someone sitting in the departments for education around the GERM world and coming up with a plan. Here is the UK's:

♦ We exhaust teachers to the point where they are too tired to think beyond the next set of marking.

♦ We vilify the unions so that even teachers don't trust them.

♦ We frighten parents into believing that there is no hope for our children unless they support the measures the government are taking to 'save' the system. We do this through the media which is owned by the people who own the tablets on which the curriculum materials they have written will be learned.

♦ We use international data to convince parents and business leaders that the education system is in crisis. To do this, we constantly mention in all of our speeches how far we are falling behind the foreigners. And in one breath, we feed the immigration fear as well.

♦ We use 'astroturfing' – the manipulation of social media through the use of multiple accounts – to create the impression of a 'dominant' viewpoint to make teachers think that their beliefs are a minority position.

These myths are now so well dispersed that everyone is playing the international comparison game. It seems that every country is peering at the others, trying to replicate what it is they do. Instead, would it not be better, as George Eliot says, to celebrate our numerous strands of experience and stop trying to cherry-pick isolated elements of practice in order to all be the same (but better).

I can understand why it would seem to make sense to look to practice elsewhere and to see what we can learn, but doing so often fails to take into consideration vast socio-cultural differences. For example, to return to Finland:

♦ Finnish teachers *are* all educated to master's level but are also drawn from the top 10% of educational achievers across the country.

♦ Finnish teachers teach on average 15.2 hours per week, leaving them time for SEN support, intervention, effective marking and continuing professional development (CPD). The average weekly teaching load of a UK teacher is 20 hours per week. (Even in Shanghai, teachers have 25% contact time with pupils – marking and planning are a priority. The same is true of Japan which frees up time for teachers to plan collaboratively through a lesson study cycle.)

While these two facts appear to be promising possible 'solutions', we should also factor in that Finland is a more monocultural society with fewer English as an additional language (EAL) children and its language has consistent phoneme/grapheme representation so that literacy is easier to achieve. Similarly, consider Malcolm Gladwell's explanation of the differences between memory of number in the English language in comparison to the Chinese language:

Chinese number words are remarkably brief. Most of them can be uttered in less than one-quarter of a second (for instance, 4 is 'si' and 7 'qi') Their English equivalents – 'four,' 'seven' – are longer: pronouncing them takes about one-third of a second. The memory gap between English and Chinese apparently is entirely due to this difference in length. ...

It turns out that there is also a big difference in how number-naming systems in Western and Asian languages are constructed. In English, we say fourteen, sixteen, seventeen, eighteen and nineteen, so one would think that we would also say one-teen, two-teen, and three-teen. But we don't. We make up a different form: eleven, twelve, thirteen, and fifteen. ... The number system in English is highly irregular. Not so in China, Japan and Korea. They have a logical counting system. Eleven is ten one. Twelve is ten two. Twenty-four is two ten four, and so on.

That difference means that Asian children learn to count much faster. Four year old Chinese children can count, on average, up to forty. American children, at that age, can only count to fifteen, and don't reach forty until they're five: by the age of five, in other words, American children are already a year behind their Asian counterparts in the most fundamental of math skills.[7]

Things are rarely as simple as they appear. We don't tend to hear about these differences in political speeches. Instead, we are inflicted with publicity stunts like bringing Chinese mathematics teachers over to the UK, as if this will actually make a difference.

Indeed, beneath the educational elements there are much more profound factors at play. For example, if we look at the common features of successful international states, cities and countries, according to both the widely quoted

---

7   Malcolm Gladwell, *Outliers: The Story of Success* (New York: Little, Brown and Co., 2008), pp. 228–229. This extract from chapter 8 is available at: http://gladwell.com/outliers/rice-paddies-and-math-tests/.

McKinsey report, *How the World's Best-Performing Schools Come Out On Top*,[8] and the OECD, they are characterised by strong teacher collaboration and opportunities for CPD, high levels of professional autonomy and greater socio-cultural equality.

According to exhaustive research in *The Spirit Level* by Richard Wilkinson and Kate Pickett, in many indices of international comparison (e.g. health, education, mental illness, crime and suicide rates) it is equality that is the indicative factor.[9] All of this combines to generate the question of what we should really be doing and why it is we're not doing it. Every indication suggests that it is social policy which narrows the gap between rich and poor and makes the most significant impact on education as well as all other areas of life.

It is not in many right leaning or even centrist governments' interests to champion the rights of the poor in policy terms. Of course, they do this through rhetoric, but the fact is that the poor across the world have been more adversely affected by the global economic downturn than the rich. Indeed, the richest have increased their wealth. While ministers accept that poverty leads to lower educational achievement, little has been done to alleviate poverty in the UK. There were 300,000 more children in poverty in 2012 than there were in 2010 (although the government's response to this shocking

---

8   Michael Barber and Mona Mourshed, *How the World's Best-Performing Schools Come Out On Top* (New York: McKinsey & Co., 2007). Available at: http://mckinseyonsociety.com/downloads/reports/Education/Worlds_School_Systems_Final.pdf.

9   Richard Wilkinson and Kate Pickett, *The Spirit Level: Why Equality is Better for Everyone* (London: Penguin, 2010).

figure was to try to redefine child poverty),[10] and a report from the Social Mobility and Child Poverty Commission in October 2013 found that two-thirds of children living in poverty were from families in work.[11] This supports similar findings in the US in 2011. It seems that taking low paid or part-time work has kept unemployment figures down but masked a growing national crisis.

Until governments begin to integrate their social and educational policies with an unrelenting focus on reducing inequality, little will be done to improve our educational standings, even in flawed international comparison tests. I'll say it again to be clear: if we want to improve education, we need to eradicate poverty. It *is* that simple. And that complicated.

In addition, there is a worrying consequence of all of this misinformation, resulting in an increasingly polarised society. We sneer at the poor and we fear the foreign. Here is an exchange from a Year 7 class as part of our work on democracy in English (it beats *Heat* magazine as a source of inspiration):

Teacher: *So have you decided on which motions you'd like to have discussed?*

The class nod.

Child 1: *Ours is, 'We should end immigration in the UK'.*

---

10 Department for Work and Pensions, *Measuring Child Poverty: A Consultation of Better Measures of Child Poverty* (November 2012). Cm. 8483 (London: The Stationery Office). Available at: https://www.gov.uk/government/uploads/system/uploads/attachment_data/file/228829/8483.pdf.

11 Social Mobility and Child Poverty Commission, *State of the Nation 2013: Social Mobility and Child Poverty in Great Britain* (London: The Stationery Office, 2013). Available at: https://www.gov.uk/government/uploads/system/uploads/attachment_data/file/292231/State_of_the_Nation_2013.pdf.

Child 2: *And ours is, 'People should not be allowed to get benefits – they should have to get a job'.*

Over the course of two 30 minute debates, there was an overwhelming belief from the children that immigrants are largely to blame for the lack of jobs in the UK and that living on benefits is a choice made by 'lazy people'. They conflate immigration with welfare, claiming that 'most immigrants come here to claim benefits'. Some go so far as to suggest that poor people should not be allowed to have children. And the poor children in the class fall silent. In such ways are George Lakoff's moral frames exhibited in classes (see Chapter 2). How often do we ignore them, tut and allow them to pass? How much time do we spend unpicking assumptions and examining how they are being created? It is simply not good enough to say, 'We don't have time' or, 'It's not in the syllabus'.

As a teacher, I clearly need to (and do) address these issues, but they expose a worrying lack of understanding, as well as evidence that these myths which are pedalled by the media are both pervasive and persuasive. Instead of gazing critically into our navels and comparing ourselves with others, we need to build more positive narratives for children. We need to move beyond neo-narcissism towards integration and a celebration of difference. And we need to fix far bigger problems than the PISA tests in order to do so.

Ten things we could teach in English and still be teaching English

1 Democracy (and the difference between direct and indirect democratic processes).

2 Interpreting data on how much money tax evasion costs us in comparison to benefits fraud.

3 Watching the BBC documentary, *Poor Kids*, and then writing letters of protest.

4 Linking up with Amnesty International and writing letters.

5 Reading Dickens and Gaskell and comparing child labour then with child labour in less economically developed countries across the world.

6 Examining Aristotle's virtue ethics and writing our own moral codes.

7 Reading Jamila Gavin's novel, *Coram Boy,* and looking at the political acts that led to the abolition of slavery and child labour in the UK/US.

8 Comparing articles written in the *Daily Mail* on immigration with the statistics and facts.

9 Setting up a mantle of the expert project to design an immigration detention centre and then role-playing a protester who thinks it might be wrong to detain refugees (especially children).

10 Getting children to write extended projects in response to questions like: Is the world a fair place? Will there always be poverty? Are human beings inherently selfish? Why do we need to compare ourselves to others?'

What has all this got to do with international comparisons? Well, if we're going to do it, let's move beyond the test. Let's move beyond a fear of all that is foreign. Let's make our comparisons affirmative, demanding and democratic. Let's educate to change the world, not to fear it.

Chapter 4

THE GAME OF CLONES: OFSTED AND ACCOUNTABILITY

A joker is a little fool who is different from everyone else. He's not a club, diamond, heart, or spade. He's not an eight or a nine, a king or a jack. He is an outsider. He is placed in the same pack as the other cards, but he doesn't belong there. Therefore, he can be removed without anybody missing him.

Jostein Gaarder, *The Solitaire Mystery* (1990)

Recently, my 6-year-old came home from school full of excitement that he was going to be having 'scooter training' the next day. He could hardly sleep and scooted into school and back out again with a big smile on his face.

'Did you enjoy that?' I asked.

'Oh, yes. It was great. It wasn't learning.'

'It was learning. I bet you learned all sorts about how to watch out for cars, stop and start, control your brakes …'

'We did all that but it wasn't learning. We were outside and there were no learning objectives.'

Across schools all over the country, little clones write objectives in their books copied from boards plastered with two letters, LO, or two words, WALT (We Are Learning Today) and WILF (What I'm Looking For). If there were ever two boys in need of expulsion they are Walt and Wilf. Even if, in every lesson, just two minutes are spent on this, that is 10 minutes per day, 50 minutes per week and 32.5 hours of learning lost per year. And that's a conservative estimate. Why do we waste this time? Because we think it is what Ofsted want. And, as a nation of teachers, we are in danger of overlooking what children need because we are relentlessly focused on providing 'evidence' for Ofsted.

The obsession with lesson objectives, like many teaching and learning fads, stems from some good advice – that children should know what it is they are learning, how best to go about it and what they need to do to improve.[1] These are the core principles on which Assessment for Learning (AfL), rooted in the work of Dylan Wiliam and Paul Black, is based. Children need to be more than passengers in their own learning. Learning needs to matter in order to stick and signposts can help. Signposts, however, are different to vehicles and WALT puts the child firmly in passenger mode – the exact mode that AfL was designed to end. This is reinforced by WILF – a confirmation that the real objective of learning is pleasing the teacher. Both WALT and WILF remove all responsibility for learning from the child. The locus of power is firmly with the teacher but so is the burden of responsibility. Even their inventor, Shirley Clarke, describes these two monsters as a blight.[2] If we want to

---

1 Paul Black and Dylan Wiliam, *Inside the Black Box: Raising Standards Through Classroom Assessment* (London: School of Education, King's College, 1998).

2 Helen Ward, Assessment for Learning Has Fallen Prey to Gimmicks, Says Critic, *TES* (15 July 2012). Available at: http://www.tes.co.uk/article.aspx?storycode=6003863.

create a generation of autonomous, responsible learners who use knowledge to make connections and who are self-motivated, then we need to kick WALT and WILF firmly into touch, along with three part lessons and making progress in 20 minutes.

The way in which AfL has been implemented in schools has been, in the words of Sue Swaffield of Cambridge University, 'a woeful waste of a wonderful opportunity'.[3] She points to the hope felt when the Labour government committed £150 million in 2008 to the development of AfL in schools, and the despair of realising that this process of 'sitting beside' a child in a formative and long term process had been reduced to a system of what Harry Torrance calls 'criteria compliance'[4] – the reduction of assessment to atomistic skills, as seen in the Assessing Pupils' Progress (APP) grids. Furthermore, the whole process of coaching a child to recognise what it is he/she needs to do to improve was reduced to simplistic and meaningless activities such as thumbs up/down and traffic lights, which are more an indication of a child's confidence than their understanding. Why is it that we teachers (and politicians) reduce valid research into vapid actions? I would argue, in large part, that it has something to do with the mindset that the only thing that matters

----

3   Sue Swaffield, The Misrepresentation of Assessment for Learning and the Woeful Waste of a Wonderful Opportunity. Paper presented at the Association for Achievement and Improvement through Assessment National Conference, Bournemouth, 16–18 December 2009. Available at: http://cdn.aaia.org.uk/content/uploads/2010/07/The-Misrepresentation-of-Assessment-for-Learning1.pdf.

4   Harry Torrance, Assessment As Learning? How the Use of Explicit Learning Objectives, Assessment Criteria and Feedback in Post-Secondary Education and Training Can Come to Dominate Learning, *Assessment in Education* 14(3) (2007): 281–294. Available at: http://www.academia.edu/3488529/Assessment_as_learning_How_the_use_of_explicit_learning_objectives_assessment_criteria_and_feedback_in_post-secondary_education_and_training_can_come_to_dominate_learning/, p. 282.

is the 20 minutes you might be seen by an inspector once every four or five years, and how this drives a snapshot mentality of teaching and learning which has been encouraged and reinforced by fearful senior management teams across the country.

It seems that we are in the midst of an epidemic of backside covering, wasting countless hours of our own and our children's time ensuring that we are seen to be doing what we think we should be doing. And, in the process, we are undermining the learning that we are charged with delivering. Where on earth do these ideas about what constitutes good practice in the classroom come from? Ofsted reports. Not from Ofsted guidance to inspectors, but from innocuous comments by inspectors who mention in passing something they saw and which is then seized on as if it is the 'only' way to do things. Before we know it, every school is doing it and even the inspectors start to see this as a 'norm'. There can be no other force in the history of education that has reduced a child's educational experience to a colourless palette of conformity in the way Ofsted have. We have moved from notions of accountability to those of recountability. We are all the same.

As a result, those maverick teachers that many of us remember fondly from our own education – the jokers in the pack – are being removed from the system. Non-compliance is not an option. It is hard to find breathing space in such systems to be your authentic teacher self. But there are pockets of air – you just need to know how to find them and use them. We need to find this unpolluted air in order to avoid the toxicity of the organisation set up to monitor schools and which has, in my opinion, restrained them to the extent that education has become a mindless experience of measurement which ironically limits growth.

Ofsted was set up in the form we might recognise it today in 1992 as part of a reorganisation of accountability systems in what was already a pervasively dominant narrative of decline. Previously schools had been inspected under a collaborative process by Her Majesty's Inspectors of Schools (HMI) inspectors, but this inspectorate was mistrusted by the Conservative government of the time, not least of all because it had roundly criticised the funding and state of school buildings.[5] Instead, when Ofsted was set up, the organisation was franchised.

Too few people understand that Ofsted is not a coherent organisation or that it is largely run by private operators whose key priority is to maintain contracts and market presence. In 2014, of 2,300 inspectors in the UK, only 300 were directly employed by Ofsted and the rest by external contractors Serco, Tribal and CfBT Education Trust – contracts worth in excess of £126 million per year. Serco also hold lucrative contracts within the prison service and both Tribal and CfBT have been accused of corruption. CfBT are the preferred academy sponsors for Lincolnshire, for example, but Ofsted have the power to fail a school and push it towards forced academy status.[6] It is rare, however, for these individual companies to come under scrutiny. Instead, the Ofsted brand carries the criticism, making it easy for future governments to 'disband' the brand while leaving the structure intact. In an attempt to homogenise the Ofsted brand, Sir Michael Wilshaw has announced an intention to increase the number of centralised HMI at Ofsted. This brings him

----

5   Gerran Thomas, Standards and School Inspection: The Rhetoric and the Reality, in Cedric Cullingford (ed.), *An Inspector Calls: Ofsted and Its Effect on School Standards* (London: Kogan Page, 1999), pp. 135–148.

6   Janet Downs, Is It Time to Call Time on Ofsted?, *Local Schools Network* (July 2012). Available at: http://www.localschoolsnetwork.org.uk/2012/07/is-it-time-to-call-time-on-ofsted/.

in direct conflict with the market driven strategies of current education policy.

When the coalition government came into office in 2010, they quickly appointed a tough talking combative figurehead committed to 'raise standards' who was unafraid of upsetting teachers. Michael and Michael looked like a match made in heaven. Yet as soon as Ofsted started producing reports showing that compared to 80% of state schools being graded 'good or above' in inspections, only 75% of free schools were, a strange anti-Ofsted narrative started to emerge not only from the left, but surprisingly, also from the right. As it became clear that 9.7% of the free schools inspected were deemed to be inadequate, in comparison to 3% of other schools, the government moved to protect the free school policy. In a leaked document, the government noted that 'political ramifications of any more free schools being judged inadequate are very high and speedy intervention is essential'.[7] It was surely no coincidence that two of the schools deemed to require improvement had been set up by Jonathan Simons, head of education at the think-tank Policy Exchange, and Tom Shinner, an adviser to Michael Gove.[8] In a very short space of time, Michael Wilshaw, the sheriff who had enjoyed the 'full confidence' of the secretary of state, was suddenly accused of becoming part of 'the Blob' – the soft, child centred ideological centre collectively known as 'enemies of promise'[9] by two leading right wing

7   Daniel Boffey and Warwick Mansell, Revealed: Gove's Bid to Limit Fallout from Failing Free Schools, *The Observer* (6 April 2014). Available at: http://www.theguardian.com/education/2014/apr/06/michael-gove-failing-free-schools.

8   Warwick Mansell, Free Schools Fail Ofsted Inspections at a Much Higher Rate Than State Schools, *The Guardian* (29 April 2014). Available at: http://www.theguardian.com/education/2014/apr/29/free-schools-ofsted-failure-rate-higher-state.

9   Gove, I Refuse to Surrender to the Marxist Teachers Hell-Bent on Destroying Our Schools.

think-tanks, one of them Policy Exchange itself. Wilshaw was outraged; Gove unrepentant. It seemed that Wilshaw would wilt, but in the end it was Michael Gove who was pushed out of office. Across the country, teachers wondered what it would mean for them. The truth is it doesn't matter. Those opening champagne on Michael Gove's departure were left only with the hungover realisation that you need to change the policy not the person in order to effect change.

What we see in Ofsted is everything that can go wrong in a target driven culture of high stakes accountability. It is easy to blame them but they are, in fact, little more than a symptom of the culture of mistrust surrounding our public services. Under data driven pressure, human beings will focus on the maintenance of the data over reality – often at the expense of the end user. We have seen this in the NHS, in education and social services. Many schools have moved away from focusing on children to focusing on our own survival as institutions, leaders and teachers. This has led to some highly unethical practices, fuelling the charge of teachers as 'cheats' without bothering to engage with the cause. It may be true that for most of the past decade, teachers and schools have been engaged in a dangerous 'What are Ofsted looking for?' game in which the only winners have been consultants and organisations selling courses with the word 'outstanding' in them. But if Ofsted are removed, and the targets and focus on results remain, the game will continue. We need to think beyond whether or not Ofsted remains or is reformed.

Ofsted is dangerously flawed but it is not progressive ideology that is causing the problems, rather it is the obsession with measuring only what is easy to measure and the impact that this has on policy and practices in schools. While Policy

Exchange and Civitas, both ardent supporters of GERM focused policies, chose to focus on what was laughably described as a 'progressive ideology' by Ofsted, the think-tank Demos released a report in May 2013, which claimed that the organisation had completely lost the confidence of the profession and labelled it as 'toxic'.[10] Instead, Demos proposed a system in which parents and pupils had a greater say in how their school was measured:

A system where all interested parties – leaders, teachers, students, parents and inspectors – have a say would be a step in the right direction. It would represent a crucial move away from a target-obsessed culture to a more balanced, trusting and effective education system.[11]

Interestingly, they also proposed a measurement of where pupils end up (i.e. education/employment) in order to ensure that schools refocus on the child's life beyond examinations. Professor Robert Coe, in his address to researchED in June 2013, also questioned the effectiveness of Ofsted, accusing them of being 'part of the problem not the solution' but also accusing teachers of being 'spineless in the way they cower to Ofsted'.[12] It is an interesting point: to what extent are we teachers the architects of our own oppression? Indeed, this tendency of ours to cling to

10 James Park, *Detoxifying School Accountability* (London: Demos, 2013). Available at: http://www.demos.co.uk/files/Detoxifying_School_Accountability_-_web.pdf?1367602207.

11 James Park quoted in, Demos: Scrap Ofsted Inspections to Tackle 'Target-Obsessed Culture' in Schools (press release, n.d.). Available at: http://www.demos.co.uk/press_releases/demosscrapofstedinspectionstotackletargetobsessedcultureinschools.

12 Robert Coe, Practice and Research in Education: How Can We Make Both Better, and Better Aligned? Paper presented at researchED Midlands, June 2013. Video available at: http://www.researched2013.co.uk/professor-robert-coe-at-researched-2013/.

structures that have been removed, such as APP, levelling and so on, is a source of great frustration to government. During the panel discussion at the 2014 Northern Rocks education conference in Leeds, former chief adviser to Michael Gove, Dominic Cummings, expressed disbelief that teachers and head teachers were not embracing the 'freedoms' that were on offer.[13] It was, of course, pointed out to him that it is difficult to walk out of prison when the dogs of data are pacing outside on the pavement. What was clear, however, was that on both left and right, there is now a wide acceptance that Ofsted, and, in particular, the labelling of lessons as 'outstanding' or otherwise, is a problem.

Under attack from all sides of the political spectrum, it is hard to see how the brand of Ofsted will survive, at least in its current form. Dame Alison Peacock, in her exploration of the role of a Royal College of Teachers, has called for the head of the teaching inspectorate to be monitored by this proposed independent professional body, which would also have influence over the appointment of the head of the organisation.[14] This would remove the pressure to meet the demands of transient secretaries of state. Whatever the solution, it is clear that changes to Ofsted now seem inevitable.

In early 2014, in response to evidence on the unreliability of classroom observations, Ofsted clarified that they would no longer grade individual lessons but rather focus their teaching and learning grading on 'progress over time'.[15] Indeed,

----

13 Dominic Cummings, Northern Rocks: Reclaiming Pedagogy, Leeds Metropolitan University, 7 June 2014.

14 Alison Peacock, *Towards a Royal College of Teaching: Raising the Status of the Profession* (London: Royal College of Surgeons of England, 2013).

15 Tom Sherrington, Meeting Ofsted: The Game Has Changed, *Headguruteacher* (20 February 2014). Available at: http://headguruteacher.com/2014/02/20/meeting-ofsted/.

Michael Cladingbowl, Ofsted's National Director of Schools, has now announced that Ofsted will trial a pilot scheme of not grading lessons at all in the West Midlands in 2014/15, with a view to this being rolled out nationwide at a later date.[16] There will be more soft touch inspections for those schools already deemed to be good and the focus will be on progress and data. We should be wary of the consequences of this. While most teachers might breathe a sigh of relief, this will push the pressure to teach to the test and produce results even further up the agenda. And many head teachers will not be happy to relinquish the observation process.

Despite compelling evidence to the contrary,[17] the myth that graded observations are secure ways of measuring the quality of teaching and learning prevails. We view our professional selves merely in terms of the unreliable grades we are given in response to small fragments of our lessons. Moreover, in too many schools, observations are not made simply to ascertain teacher quality but to ensure consistent application of school policies and practices. As Robert Coe points out, there are too many confused agendas driving observations.[18] At worst, these form part of a surveillance culture that rates compliance over creativity and individuality.

As teachers, we have exacerbated all of the above every single time we have tweeted or Facebooked a gleeful 'I got outstanding!' message. Worse, we have beaten ourselves up

---

16 Michael Cladingbowl, *Why I Want To Try Inspecting Without Grading Teaching In Each Individual Lesson* (4 June 2014). Ref: 140101. Available at: http://www.ofsted.gov.uk/resources/why-i-want-try-inspecting-without-grading-teaching-each-individual-lesson.

17 Andrew Ho and Thomas Kane, *The Reliability of Classroom Observations by School Personnel* (Seattle, WA: Bill & Melinda Gates Foundation, 2013). Available at: http://www.metproject.org/downloads/MET_Reliability_of_Classroom_Observations_Research_Paper.pdf.

18 Coe, Practice and Research in Education.

every time we are told we require improvement and slip into misery. We turn against our colleagues who are 'better than' or 'worse than' ourselves. We turn against our managers. We shout abuse at Ofsted. Like wounded animals, we snarl and attack and lick our wounds. And this drains our energy to the extent that we no longer have the ability to think about how things might be different. As a divide and conquer strategy it is unparalleled.

Before we celebrate the potential demise of the classroom observation, or of Ofsted, we should consider the implications of the alternative. Data is now not only king but queen, prince and peasant. In the Kingdom of Accountability the whole picture will focus on progress. And this is dangerous. No child will be allowed to fall off our neat, linear progress path. Instead of acknowledging that learning is not linear, this notion will be reinforced. We already push staff through countless stressful, summative 'mocksteds', work scrutinies and data analyses instead of providing formative peer support and mentoring. We have lost school plays, trips and events to make way for exam preparation. We have long encouraged our staff to play the system in order to secure results that will play to the accountability measures, leaping through whatever hoops are deemed necessary. And now the hoop is a lot smaller: shorter, more frequent inspection visits focusing relentlessly on progress made. Anyone familiar with the work of economist Steven Levitt will tell you where this leads.[19] If you force people to meet targets and make the stakes high enough, many of them will do anything, and I mean *anything*, to perform.

Whether it is an act as outrageous as falsifying coursework or the case of the 'outstanding teacher' who repeats a lesson

----

19 Steven Levitt and Stephen Dubner, *Freakonomics: A Rogue Economist Explores the Hidden Side of Everything* (New York: William Morrow, 2005).

three or four times in the hope of 'catching' the inspector (this teacher was rewarded with a promotion by their senior management team), there is a rife system of game playing. But before we start bashing and berating the profession, let's take stock for a moment. This is a mess of the government's making, of both red and blue hues, and stems from two decades of mistrust. Put people in chains and some will behave like criminals. Others will plod along. Some will complain and a few will revolt. Tightening the chains will not solve the problem. Freedom solves the problem, as is proven in education systems with high levels of teacher autonomy. This idea that autonomy breeds responsibility and creativity is what underpins the work of Daniel Pink, who points to research that this is a human phenomenon across all cultures and age groups.[20] If it is true, then it stands to reason that autonomy and trust are the corner-stones of a functional system of accountability.

I am not arguing for the abolition of Ofsted, or at least not until our system has undergone a radical overhaul in terms of teacher training, assessment and curriculum design, but instead I ask what a good inspectorate might look for. What if an outstanding school could only be outstanding if:

♦ They committed to offering teaching placements to students (as hospitals do). This would reduce the scramble of universities and other organisations 'begging' for places to be offered to their students.

♦ There was a wide reaching commitment to extracurricular activity and that this activity was encouraged by senior leaders who reduced meeting times after school and allowed teachers with a large load of extra duties (e.g. PE and performing arts staff) to have reduced

---

20 Daniel Pink, *Drive: The Surprising Truth About What Motivates Us* (New York: Riverhead, 2009).

timetables in order to have the energy and time to commit to this role. (Look at Eton which employs external coaches/directors specifically for the purpose.) Money? Stop spending your budgets on mocksteds.

♦ There was a thriving culture of cultural/educational trips for pupils, facilitated by admin staff who took the load off teachers in planning, booking and risk assessing the trips.

♦ Progress took into account the child's developments in confidence, speech and managing their physical and emotional needs as well as academic performance.

♦ Every child had full access to a broad and balanced curriculum and was not simply receiving an intensive and limiting diet of intervention (which rarely works).

Most of the things in this list are deemed to be luxuries in the eyes of many school leaders, but thinkers such as E. D. Hirsch[21] and others point to the vital importance of cultural literacy and vocabulary in developing a learner. Tim Brighouse suggests a list of non-negotiable entitlements for all children, incorporating trips, sporting events, a residential visit, community service and universal access to the internet/e-learning platforms hosted by universities.[22] Such an entitlement would allow a child to understand the best of the culture and history of mankind. Visiting galleries, museums and theatres can have significant impact – I'll never forget being taken by my beloved music teacher to the Free Trade Hall in Manchester to see an orchestra for the first time in my life. It blew my mind and Rachmaninov's Piano

---

21 E. D. Hirsch, *The Knowledge Deficit: Closing the Shocking Education Gap for American Children* (New York: Houghton Mifflin, 2006).

22 Tim Brighouse, All I Want for Education, *The Guardian* (2 January 2009). Available at: http://www.theguardian.com/education/2009/jan/02/tim-brighouse-wishlist.

Concerto No. 2 has stayed in my heart for thirty years. All children should be entitled to see, hear and experience the best that our culture has to offer as part of their education. Too often, these experiences are lost to the endless chasing of data.

In our school, the emphasis on 'progress over time' has led to a re-examination of the way we record data and a focus on looking at the marking in books. There is a renewed obsession with levels, even as they have supposedly disappeared. Judging from the feedback at our local teaching and learning network group, this is leading to some highly questionable practices, such as observers demanding that pupils make at least one sub-level of progress in a lesson. If it were possible to do this, every Year 9 pupil in the country would have a PhD! Our local schools are deeply reluctant to replace levels because of the fear that they will be unable to show progress. Instead of focusing on developing formative feedback processes, schools are having energy drained from them trying to figure out how they will demonstrate progress at a national level without levels and grades. Writers like Daisy Christodoulou are right to point out that getting rid of levels is an opportunity for schools to be genuinely focused on what a child can do and know;[23] the inhibitor, ironically, is the system that claims to ensure quality.

When these types of statistics are scrutinised, the teacher feels under pressure to input data that seem to show progress. When I was adding half-termly data into our tracking system at the beginning of the year, I was warned by colleagues not to show too much progress for the pupils, in case they fell back and 'it looked bad'. Elsewhere, some

---

23 Daisy Christodoulou, Why National Curriculum Levels Need Replacing, *The Wing to Heaven* (3 April 2014). Available at: http://thewingtoheaven. wordpress.com/2014/04/03/why-national-curriculum-levels-need-replacing/.

pupils look like they've stayed the same and some look like they've fallen backwards. The problem is that we're measuring different things all the time. The spreadsheet doesn't allow me to say that one child's mother was diagnosed with cancer or that we were assessing technical writing ability at one point and speaking and listening at another. Crude instruments do not allow for a rich timbre, and at the moment our instruments are screeching. We think we're showing progress but we're just making a noise.

Unpopular as it may sound, therefore, getting rid of Ofsted will not work on its own. And neither will getting rid of the flawed graded observations. Both might relieve the stress of the teacher, of course, but it would not improve education for pupils. Schools will be held accountable with or without Ofsted. Consider the impact of the judgement being based on nothing more than league tables. Where might that path lead us?

We need a philosophical revolution, not a simple reform of a body no longer fit for purpose. We need to re-evaluate our dependency on examinations, on certainty, on the belief that trying again (and again) is not the path to success but is cheating (bin all those Robert the Bruce stories, boys and girls!). We need to ask: Would we rather have a generation of children who become literate and numerate eventually or a generation where some do and some don't? Would we rather have a nation of resilient people who keep on trying or a nation of successes and failures divided by their performance on a single day of their lives? Would we rather have a system that offers second chances to all? Will the world end if some children take longer to reach a point of competency? Of course not, it will be better. And universities looking to recruit only nailed-it-first-time-with-the-help-of-the-thousands-of-pounds-my-parents-spent-on-private-tuition students can have them. There will be employers aplenty who will snap up the plodder who kept on trying and got there in the end.

For this to happen, schools cannot be judged on the results of a single year group in examinations in a single year. Progress 8 measures are a better indicator than 5 A–Cs but only if we find secure ways of ensuring that children are able to show their best performance. And while we wait for that to happen, here's something you can do right now.

(R)evolutionary practice

◆ Be your authentic teacher self. Make sure that you keep up to date with the latest research and thinking on education but then make this work for you. Never do anything because someone tells you it is what Ofsted want. When you hear this, ask for the research or theory underpinning the idea.

◆ Never ask for a grade after an observation. Simply ask for something that you did well and the key area for improvement. We *all* require improvement, even those who are deemed outstanding with a touch of spaceship (to borrow from Hywel Roberts[24]).

◆ If greatness is thrust upon you and your grade is offered despite your protestations, resist all temptation to brag about it. You can tell your parents if you must.

◆ If you are told that your lesson was not good enough, take control of your situation. Ask for a reading list and set up a series of observations where you watch your

---

24 Hywel Roberts, *Oops! Helping Children Learn Accidentally* (Carmarthen: Independent Thinking Press, 2012).

observer teach. Make it clear that you will not learn simply by being re-observed in ten days' time. You need a clearly defined set of opportunities to watch others work, to co-plan and to research. You are entitled to support not sanctions. Ultimately, remember that an inspection looks first and foremost at what the learners are learning. Shift your focus from yourself to them and try to see the learning through their eyes.

♦ Remember that there is no evidence whatsoever that Ofsted observation models are a reliable indicator of your competence as a teacher.[25]

♦ Think about yourself as a learner. What drives you mad in staff INSET sessions? Are you guilty of delivering the same diet to pupils that you rebel against when it is done to you? If you start to fume when being told that you must do (learn) something you disagree with or don't see the point of, then think about how a child feels when they can't see the relevance of the learning. What would win you round? Can you apply this to your teaching?

♦ Never do anything that is not in the best interests of the children. Others may disagree but if you argue from positions of integrity, rather than self-interest, you have a chance of making a difference.

♦ Use Twitter and blogs to share your stories of inconsistencies and absurdities. The more public the forum, the more attention the problem gets.

---

25 Professor Robert Coe quoted in Judith Burns, Ofsted Methods May Not Be Valid, Says Senior Academic, BBC News (13 September 2013). Available at: http://www.bbc.co.uk/news/education-24079951.

Then reform

♦ Campaign for an accountability system led by teachers through a professional teacher body at arm's length from government. Proposals for a Royal or Chartered College of Teaching could be an answer to the Ofsted problem, especially if it has the power to appoint inspectors.

♦ Recognise that accountability, when done well, is both necessary and healthy – like good assessment, it is formative. As a senior manager, consider what formative accountability would look like for your staff. As staff, recognise that it is part of your professional duty to be informed, reflective and proactive in seeking to improve your practice.

♦ Build collaborative observation and co-planning systems into your school – Japanese lesson study is a great way forward.[26]

♦ Encourage peer-to-peer observation based on a 'what went well' and 'even better if' mentality. In short, apply the same formative assessment processes to staff that you would apply to children.

♦ Move your classroom practice and whole school systems away from 'predictive trust' environments to 'vulnerability based trust' environments.[27] In a nutshell, that means instead of only trusting those who have played our game the way we wanted it to be played, we trust from a posi-

---

26 Phil Wood and Wasyl Cajkler, Beyond Communities of Practice: Investigating and Developing the Professional Learning of Trainee Teachers Through Lesson Study. Research report for the Society for Educational Studies (2013). Available at: http://www.soc-for-ed-studies.org.uk/documents/smallgrants/finalReports/wood-and-cajkler.pdf.

27 Patrick Lencioni, The Five Dysfunctions of a Team: A Leadership Fable (Garden City, NY: Wiley, 2002).

tion of vulnerability. This means accepting that people will make mistakes, that almost all can improve, that 'there but for the grace of God go I' and that sharing errors and rectifying them without judgement builds better performance. In the words of Dylan Wiliam, 'no teacher is so good that they can't be better'.[28]

♦ As Ian Gilbert once said to me, 'Let the data serve the children. Never let the children serve the data.'

---

28 Quoted in Stephanie Sparrow, Classroom Craftsman [an interview with Dylan Wiliam], *Make the Grade* (Spring 2008): 25–27. Available at: http://www.dylanwiliam.org/Dylan_Wiliams_website/Bios_files/CIEA%20 interview.pdf.

Chapter 5

TEACHING: NOT FOR LILY PAD HOPPERS

That sir which serves and seeks for gain,

And follows but for form,

Will pack when it begins to rain,

And leave thee in the storm,

But I will tarry; the fool will stay,

And let the wise man fly:

The knave turns fool that runs away;

The fool no knave, perdy.

Shakespeare, *King Lear*, Act 2, Scene 4

I had always wanted to be a teacher until I went to university and heard one too many people tell me I was too clever to teach. So I went into advertising and PR instead, where I met many very stupid people. Writing a press release which attempted to play down the impending redundancies of my colleagues was a particular high point of that career, so I moved into marketing – as a marketing director, no less – which really involved selling accessories for cars and bicycles. Apparently, I was too clever for teaching and was destined to persuade Halfords to buy extending handled, strap-on bike racks instead. Of course, this was not time wasted: I learned the invaluable skills of duplicity and persuasion, but eventually I embarked on my vocation by enrolling on a PGCE at a Russell Group university.

I would like to be able to say that my experience of PGCE cemented for me the importance of the university in the role of shaping teachers of the future. But I can't. The course was rubbish – on placement I was pretty much left to fend for myself. I learned, as anyone does, by bumbling along. But I only learned to survive. Sessions in university were patchy and often the information we had found ourselves was more up to date than that given to us by our lecturers. Sometimes our lecturers were not present and we ran the sessions ourselves. But then this was before Ofsted and the Training and Development Agency (TDA) became involved in regulating and properly inspecting teacher training provision. When I returned to university as an initial teacher training (ITT) tutor, I found a very different world. It was a salutary lesson in not judging something on the experience you had yourself. Having said that, I would still argue that the PGCE is inadequate preparation for teaching. But then so are the alternatives.

This chapter explores what might be done about teacher training. As far as primary school training is concerned, I take it as read that the comprehensive four-year-long BEd degree programme is the best preparation for teaching. The course covers all aspects of subject knowledge as well as psychology, child development, research and pedagogy. This chapter focuses on postgraduate provision.

Fractured by fear

The current system of teacher training in the UK has been fractured beyond recognition by a fear that universities are hotbeds of subversion that have fed the union movement. This 'Marxist Blob' nightmare has been repeated ad infinitum across both sides of the Atlantic, feeding the belief that the problem with education is, well … the educated. A cosy little group of neo-liberal advocates have fed this myth, supported by a body of opinion that the 'problem' with education lies in the fact that all academics are in thrall to Rousseau and romantic notions of child led learning.[1] This narrative is becoming pervasive, and yet when we look at its sources we see a number of trends emerging. Firstly, many of the texts produced promoting the idea of a dangerous 'Blob' come from a narrow ideological field. The first, Daisy Christodoulou's *Seven Myths About Education*, was published by the Curriculum Centre, an organisation set up to support E. D. Hirsch's proposals for a core curriculum and which is supported by Michael Gove and Civitas. The second, an inflammatory pamphlet by controversial journalist Toby Young,[2] was published by Civitas, the right wing think-tank which publishes guides to E. D. Hirsch's curriculum model. The third, *Progressively Worse*, was written by Robert Peal,[3] a TeachFirst graduate who fled the classroom as soon as his training was over to become an educational consultant with … Civitas, who also published his book. This does not,

----

1 Daisy Christodoulou, *Seven Myths About Education* (Abingdon: Routledge / Curriculum Centre, 2014).

2 Toby Young, *Prisoners of the Blob: Why Most Education Experts Are Wrong About Nearly Everything* (London: Civitas, 2014).

3 Robert Peal, *Progressively Worse: The Burden of Bad Ideas in British Schools* (London: Civitas, 2014).

however, dampen the publicity surrounding the publications, which is supported by a large 'astroturfing' community.

Secondly, the trend for astroturfing has been a dominant tool in promoting the GERM ideology in US education and now it is becoming pervasive here. It involves the manipulation of social media to create the impression of, say, Twitter support for a policy when, in fact, the supporters hold more than one account – in some cases several hundred. This creates a belief among teachers and parents that their views or experiences are in a minority, and public opinion has shifted. If these practices are enhanced with high profile book launches and mentions in the speeches of government ministers, then this only enhances the effect. To this end, and with these methods, universities and teachers' unions have been undermined.

Thirdly, it would seem that the word 'progressive' has become tainted with the charge of weakness, while the words 'child centred' are bandied around as if they are a curse. George Lakoff points out that the values of progressive thinking are 'empathy, interdependence, co-operation, communication, authority that is legitimate and proves its legitimacy with its openness to interrogation'.[4] Progressive thinkers do not reject authority but we do argue for an open legitimacy. This is quite different to the narrative being fed to us by these right wing writers.

Fourthly, universities, it would seem, are dangerous hotbeds of progressive thinking. The reality is that universities live in fear: the fear of student numbers being cut, making courses and jobs unviable. Sometimes the numbers of

---

4   George Lakoff quoted in Zoe Williams, George Lakoff: 'Conservatives Don't Follow the Polls, They Want to Change Them ... Liberals Do Everything Wrong', *The Guardian* (1 February 2014). Available at: http://www. theguardian.com/books/2014/feb/01/george-lakoff-interview.

places on teaching courses that the universities can offer (and which are set by government) change several times throughout the recruitment process. Over the past few years, this has resulted in a farce with universities and candidates caught up in a bewildering mess of changing allocations. The universities get a reputation for being badly organised while the real root cause of the farce remains unidentified. Despite the fact that there is an impending teacher shortage, successive governments have failed to recognise the need for stability and independence in the teacher training sector. Worse, in recent years, relentless attacks from government on those who question policy have led to a situation in which academics are now seen as enemies not only of the state but of children. At the same time, the Department for Education is calling for research led education.[5] It is unclear how this can take place if academics are deemed to be the enemy.

In order to understand initial teacher training better, there are a couple of things that need to be grasped. Firstly, there are separations in many universities between educational research units and ITT provision. ITT tutors may or may not publish academic research, they are usually teachers or ex-head teachers and they form the point of liaison between academic study and in-school training. Both tutors and the universities are in thrall to two accountability drivers: Ofsted and the newly qualified teacher (NQT) survey, which can trigger inspection or government intervention.

Since 2007, government priority for education has been pushed on to universities relentlessly and punitively, and the accountability for whether or not these priorities have

---

5 Ben Goldacre, *Building Evidence into Education* (London: Department for Education, 2013). Available at: http://media.education.gov.uk/assets/files/pdf/b/ben%20goldacre%20paper.pdf.

been delivered comes through the questions set by government in the form of the NQT survey. Unsurprisingly, then, the questions are politically loaded. During this period, the main focus for primary provision in the UK has been the delivery of phonics. When I was a tutor for literacy at Manchester Metropolitan University, it was expected that I would evidence teaching of phonics in every single session. This is a far cry from Nick Gibb's assertion that the 'problem' with education is 'academics in the educational faculties of universities' who he claims have set up 'opposition to the use of phonics in the teaching of young children to read'.[6] Let's be clear: ITT tutors have always advocated the teaching of phonics as part of the process of learning to read. The controversy surrounds the belief that synthetic phonics alone will provide the answer, and that particular debate takes place not in ITT sessions in universities but in academic journals.

On the ground, I found that sessions traditionally set aside for exploring the breadth of children's literature and reading for pleasure made way for phonics. Sessions on poetry made way for phonics. Sessions on SEN made way for phonics. Sessions on behaviour made way for phonics. Then, in 2009, we were told that APP was the main priority (in addition to phonics). The curriculum for literacy was squashed into two areas: early reading and assessment. The result was a squeeze on the foundation subjects – geography, history, languages, arts, PE and so on lost time to make way for the emphasis on APP.

Academics who knew of research questioning the wisdom of such a narrow approach were silenced. We could not

---

6   Nick Gibb, Teaching Unions Aren't the Problem – Universities Are, *The Guardian* (23 April 2014). Available at: http://www.theguardian.com/commentisfree/2014/apr/23/teaching-unions-arent-problem-universities-schools-minister?CMP=twt_gu#start-of-comments.

openly voice our concerns in front of students, or at least not in a way that would allow for proper time to examine the evidence. There was no time for critical engagement or debate. In spite of all of this, student satisfaction results showed that our NQTs were still not rating their preparation for teaching phonics highly enough and this one question alone was enough to trigger further investigation from Ofsted and the TDA. It turns out that the question confused students. It asked how 'confident' students felt in the teaching of synthetic phonics, and most of our lovely and humble students lacked confidence not ability. In such ways are perceptions formed. We decided that it was therefore going to be necessary to spend a little time (which could have been spent exploring literature) teaching our students how to interpret the questions on the survey. 'Doh!' said our colleagues from other universities, 'Had you not done that already?' Then, in December 2013, Ofsted announced that reading literature for pleasure was not being done properly in schools – the very thing we'd had to remove in order to accommodate the new thing is now the new thing. And the whirligig of time brings in his revenges.

Elsewhere, in secondary provision, similar pressures were brought to bear in which the key priority on every course was to prepare students to understand the policy of the day, the assessment structures of the day and the curriculum content of the day. Vital areas such as pedagogy, educational research, cognitive science, neuroscience, behaviour management and SEN were side-lined in order to ensure orders were followed. In such ways have universities largely become the puppets of government and in such ways are academics and tutors silenced.

Of course, all over the country, many try to resist and find opportunities where they can to open up discussion and debate, but too often these are asides and are dismissed by worried young trainees as irrelevant. The significance of theory often does not become apparent until years later when the cry goes up, 'Why did we never learn any of this at university?' Well, now you know. So, what are the alternatives?

TeachFirst

TeachFirst was inspired by Teach for America in the US. Emerging from a successful pilot project called London First, the programme is founded on the idea of persuading high flying graduates from top universities to give teaching a go. They commit for two years, and if it doesn't work out they're free to leave. Strong partnership links with blue chip companies means that there is reassurance for some that managerial level positions will be found elsewhere once time is served. For many schools, two years with a bright novice is far preferable to constant teacher absence and turnover, as was endemic in many inner city schools. In times of economic difficulty, when graduate recruitment is at an all-time low, TeachFirst is an attractive prospect for graduates looking to ride the storm. But how effective is that strategy for the profession in the long term?

There are some compelling benefits to TeachFirst. Research by Becky Allen at the Institute of Education and Jay Allnutt (a TeachFirst graduate) suggests that the programme has had an impact on the GCSE scores of children in schools who take TeachFirst trainees (although they cannot separate out other factors such as strong leadership).[7] Even the most hard pressed cynic would find it difficult to argue that TeachFirst has not brought some significant and positive change to some of our most challenging schools. In addition, there are some excellent elements to the principles and structure of the programme:

♦ A strong team ethos, with ongoing opportunities for collaboration and support.

♦ High levels of recruitment from top graduates who may never have otherwise considered teaching.

♦ The backing of industry, with high levels of sponsorship and funding for ongoing CPD and recruitment to teaching.

♦ A commitment to research in education delivered through ongoing networking and training.

I know advocates of TeachFirst would list many more but that's their job, not mine. TeachFirst spent over £2,384,427 in 2012 on ambassadors to push the message and a further £5,229,396 on recruitment alone.[8] Critics of the recruitment tactics of TeachFirst point to how this money is used to fund addresses at conferences (TeachFirst ambassadors have a disproportionately high presentation profile at events such as the Festival of Education and researchED) and to target university undergraduates, thereby undermining alternative PGCE provision. As a result, instead of becoming an addition or enhancement to current

---

7   Rebecca Allen and Jay Allnutt, Matched Panel Data Estimates of the Impact of TeachFirst on School and Departmental Performance. Department of Quantitative Social Science Working Paper No. 13-11 (2013). Available at: http://repec.ioe.ac.uk/REPEc/pdf/qsswp1311.pdf.

8   TeachFirst, *Annual Review 2012/13* (London: TeachFirst, 2013). Available at: http://www.teachfirst.org.uk/sites/default/files/ar/pdf/Annual%20 Review%202013%20web.pdf, p. 47.

provision, we end up with competition on an un-level playing field. Universities simply cannot compete with that amount of promotional spending.

According to data from the Education Select Committee, it costs almost £7,000 per year more to train a TeachFirst teacher than a PGCE teacher, although this figure does not factor in expenditure on recruitment, fundraising or the ambassador programme, which brings the cost up by a further £4,166 per candidate.[9] Some of this cost is met by fundraising but much is covered by government grants and contributions from schools. As such, the benefits that TeachFirst bring are largely achievable because of additional funding. There is no way of knowing how successful university provision would be with an equivalent level of funding. (Though one PGCE student at the Institute of Education, University of London remarked wryly, 'You know when the TeachFirst lot are coming in – they have tables of canapés in their room.')

It is not my intention here to argue that we should spend less on TeachFirst, but that if we are to have an outstanding profession then we should spend the same on all student teachers. It is also divisive that while PGCE students incur costs of £9,000 per year to train, TeachFirst graduates are paid to train, allowing them to be able to afford to remain in city centres. (London fares better in this respect as it would seem that many graduates prefer to do their teaching time in the capital.)

Two of the most commonly raised objections to the programme, however, are flawed. Firstly, although John Hattie

---

9   House of Commons Education Committee, *Great Teachers: Attracting, Training and Retaining the Best. Ninth Report on Session 2010–12*. Ref: HC 1515-II (London: The Stationery Office, 2012). Available at: http://www.publications. parliament.uk/pa/cm201012/cmselect/cmeduc/1515/1515ii.htm.

and Greg Yates point to the problem that a subject expert can have an empathy gap, having forgotten the complexity of the learning of his/her subject,[10] the argument that brilliant graduate = poor empathy misses the rigour of the selection process. It is not easy to get on to a TeachFirst course and attacking those who do is to undermine the effort and achievement of winning that place.

The second objection is that it is not possible to prepare for teaching in a hothoused six week course over the summer holiday and then to throw a trainee into one of the most challenging schools in the country. It is hard to argue against this but, hour for hour, TeachFirst graduates get as much CPD input as university based PGCE students when this six weeks is added to the two year ongoing training, usually delivered by a PGCE tutor. In short, the amount of training a TeachFirst student gets is not that different to a PGCE student. Neither gets enough. This shortage of in depth pedagogical training is a problem across both models. But both offer far more than the woefully inadequate alternatives – school based training or unqualified status.

I find myself torn between the benefits and the inequality, but there are some significant problems with TeachFirst, not least of all with the name. First before what? Before something better? Before something more lucrative? Even founder Brett Wigdortz admits that the name (and its subsequent connotations) was a 'mistake'.[11] While the retention rate for TeachFirst is not much worse than other routes, the published figures are slightly misleading. TeachFirst state that 67% of their trainees are still 'involved in education' five years later, but this does not mean that they are still

10 John Hattie and Greg Yates, *Visible Learning and the Science of How We Learn* (Abingdon: Routledge, 2013).

11 Brett Wigdortz, response to a question at the *Sunday Times* Festival of Education, Wellington College, Berkshire, 20–21 June 2014.

teachers. And these statistics are carefully managed and negotiated. One TeachFirst ambassador told me that there is a 'gentlemen's agreement' that companies will not cream off more than a third of TeachFirst graduates once training is completed, so that the retention statistics remain competitive with other routes. For ambitious trainees not in that third, there is a fast track pathway into management in schools, but this runs the risk that inexperienced teachers are in the position of grading and judging others before they have fully learned their own craft. Others leave teaching altogether and take up positions connected to education – for example, working in think-tanks, research units, the media and for TeachFirst itself – and these count within the retention statistics as they are still 'working' in education. Some are simply not wanted at the end of their training. One school in Salford let three out of four of their TeachFirst trainees go at the end of their two years – it was felt that they were not good enough.

Furthermore, I worry about the close links between the programme and government ideology (and there are few ideological differences between all three main political parties). If I was in government, it might suit me to encourage and support a young, temporary workforce, to put them in areas of teacher shortage, to keep them mobile, to use their energy before they have families and become fixed, and then replace them before they get expensive and build up pension pots. It might suit me to replace the profession with short term rapid response units who won't feel the need to be unionised because they won't be in it for long enough. I might even encourage the setting up of an alternative to the unions called Edapt and encourage TeachFirst graduates to join it. It would suit me to encourage them to support current government policy in return for a nice little advisory job at the end of it and to feed these voices to the media as 'authentic' teachers. It would suit me very much.

In recent years, TeachFirst has become increasingly connected both to the Conservative government and organisations focused on profiting from education, such as Pearson. TeachFirst, like Teach for America, is canny though. It knows that whoever is in power needs to be courted, so on both sides of the Atlantic, the organisations have been extremely successful at winning favour with parties of all colours, all of whom support, to one degree or another, the Global Education Reform Movement. The current director of research at TeachFirst is the affable Sam Freedman, who is keen to stress that he is a *former* adviser to Michael Gove. This relationship, however, has led to the increasing prominence of TeachFirst in political speeches and in the forum of social media.

More worrying is the increasing number of TeachFirst-as-a-route-to-consultancy voices across education. As such, we see the rising dominance of teachers like Daisy Christodoulou, name-checked by ministers and referred to as a 'brilliant' teacher but who, in fact, left teaching after three years. Christodoulou took up a post as a director at the Curriculum Foundation, an organisation that promotes Michael Gove's preferred 'core knowledge curriculum' model in academy schools (and is sponsored by the Tory education minister in charge of academies, Lord Nash). More recently, she became head of research at ARK, another academy chain, and is also a governor at the Michaela Free School, which is headed up by Tory darling Katherine Birbalsingh. She will be joined by prominent TeachFirst blogger Joe Kirby, also name-checked by Michael Gove and Robert Peal (aka blogger Matthew Hunter), also name-checked by … you've got it. Almost all the new heads of department appointed at the school are leading TeachFirst ambassadors. This school will not be allowed to fail. It has an adviser to the prime minister and journalists from the *Daily Mail* and *Daily Telegraph* on its governing body. Hardly a fair playing field with a state maintained school but a perfect base from which to promote policy.

None of this is to suggest that Ms Christodoulou and Co. are not without talent, but it does serve as evidence, if one is 'on message', that TeachFirst may indeed form a stepping stone to a more prominent and lucrative future. We also see recently qualified TeachFirst graduates taking up positions at Civitas and the Policy Exchange. Both organisations are ardent supporters of Conservative education policy, which further reinforces the idea that there is an increased alignment of political ideology which allows TeachFirst to be used as a weapon in the battle with universities.

Whether we have a Conservative or Labour administration, no teacher training programme should ever be closely tied to government and consultancy positions should never be offered to people with so little hands-on classroom experience. Hattie and Yates are clear that expert teachers take time to form – between five and ten years of constant reflective practice and improvement[12] – so we should not be putting novices (no matter how clever or talented) in charge of pedagogical and curriculum policy. Such incidents may seem minor but they serve to create a mood of mistrust around the TeachFirst brand – a mistrust that is undermining the good work that is being done in schools around the country. If the brand is to have credibility, it needs to become less connected to government (of any colour) and less nepotistic.

----

12 Hattie and Yates, *Visible Learning*.

Schools Direct and school-centred initial teacher training

Of course, TeachFirst alone cannot provide the sheer volume of teachers required to plug the shortage that now exists. It is necessary to train new teachers, and quickly, in order to respond to what has been an appallingly short sighted planning policy by both the last and the current government. Desperately, Michael Gove allowed academies and free schools to opt out of employing qualified teachers altogether. The Labour party vow to ensure that all teachers will be qualified to QTS level – but is this a high enough benchmark? What is it to be qualified? The bridging provision between university and being unqualified is the notion of teaching-as-apprenticeship. Enter Schools Direct and school-centred initial teacher training (SCITT) – incarnations of the former Graduate Teacher Programme. Candidates are trained on the job, sometimes as part of a cluster of schools (SCITT) or in partnership with a higher education provider (Schools Direct), and although they lead to qualified teacher status, there is no postgraduate qualification necessary to achieve the award. Engagement with educational research, pedagogical theory and critical analysis is therefore not required – flying directly in the face of evidence from the OECD that the best school systems in the world have the most highly qualified teachers. There are, of course, some areas in which this works – one SCITT partnership in Greater Manchester looks really promising and there is rigorous academic provision being offered – but there is no guarantee of consistency of quality across these models and they have struggled to recruit.

Ofsted's report into teacher training routes in 2011 over-whelmingly supported the higher education route as preferable and more rigorous than employment based routes in terms of quality. It states that their inspection process shows that 'there is proportionately less outstanding provision in employment-based routes than in HEI [higher education institution]-led partnerships'.[13]

Such reports, combined with a lack of clarity over end points and career progression and the horror stories emerging from trainees in Schools Direct programmes of being treated like supply teachers with little training or support, have led to an unexpected shortfall in the number of applicants to Schools Direct. It is this shortfall that has led to confusion and chaos in the university sector.

Despite this, successive governments have pursued a programme of undermining the professional integrity of teaching routes, not as a means to quality but as quick fixes to problems of their own making. Teacher shortages is a complex issue and sticking plaster solutions do not work. In order to attract the best into the profession, a cultural shift needs to take place and there needs to be, in my opinion, consistency across provision as a means of establishing a standard that all must reach. To get to that level of quality, two things need to change:

1 Governments need to show that teachers are respected by using supportive and positive language to describe them. Raising the status of a profession is much easier if you don't constantly criticise it. How many brilliant

---

13 Ofsted, *The Annual Report of Her Majesty's Chief Inspector of Education, Children's Services and Skills* 2010/11. Ref: HC 1633 (London: The Stationery Office). Available at: https://www.gov.uk/government/uploads/system/uploads/attachment_data/file/247177/1633.pdf, p. 76.

footballers want to play for Accrington Stanley? Talk our profession up.

2   The profession needs to work towards building relation-ships with the media so that a range of opinions is expressed. Too often, the media will call on reliable stal-warts for comments (people with much more time on their hands than a teacher, like a journalist or think-tank consultant). Teachers need to be authentically heard – this requires engaging with the media and managing our PR. The besmirching of the unions has meant that a statement from them is often less helpful to the image of teachers than it might be, no matter how sensible the comment. This is one critical area that a professional body, such as a Royal College of Teachers, could effec-tively manage.

If the status of the teaching profession was raised to the point that it was a laudable and aspirational goal to be a teacher (not an act of charity or a stop gap), that it was com-petitive, highly regarded and demanding, and if all routes into teaching were equally funded and qualified, then we would not have to keep inventing ways to entice people in. We would not have to resort to bribery.

We are potentially creating a situation where our schools are manned by teachers who will never achieve expertise as they simply won't be around long enough to do so. There are both economic and political motivations for going down this route. Young teachers are less likely to strike, they are less likely to become expensive and they are more likely to move for work. These are all attractive propositions for gov-ernment. But teachers who stay pay.

At the same time, governments in all countries in recent years have become obsessed with their nation's standing in international comparison tests. This is a subject of another chapter (see Chapter 3), but if we look at the features that the OECD claim are common to high achieving countries in terms of teacher training, we find that:

♦ Teaching as a profession is held in high status across society.

♦ Teachers are very highly qualified. In Finland, teacher training is more difficult to access than law or medicine and all teachers hold master's level qualifications.

♦ Experience is highly valued.

♦ Teachers in high achieving countries have high levels of autonomy.

The 2007 McKinsey report concluded that teacher quality was the single most important factor in securing educational success.[14] Teacher training cannot be ignored or delivered on the cheap. Neither can ongoing CPD and teacher collaboration. So, what can be done about teacher training?

---

14 Barber and Mourshed, *How the World's Best-Performing Schools Come Out On Top*.

A teaching revolution

- Move all teacher training back into universities and give universities autonomy over content.

- Make all teacher training courses a two year postgraduate qualification with master's level end points. These two years might come after a three year BEd programme or another form of degree.

- A two year programme could be done in partnership with a leading school – perhaps a teaching school alliance in order to ensure quality provision of placements.

- Ensure that any school hoping to be graded good or outstanding by Ofsted offers teacher training placements. The crisis over quality placements in schools is a significant problem for universities, so we need to shift towards a culture of obligation for training new teachers.

- ITT provision in universities should be staffed by academics who can demonstrate their practice in the classroom. This could be achieved by having 'university schools' where the teaching is delivered, in part, by staff from the university or programmes in which university staff regularly teach in partner schools. Like any education system, its quality is dependent on its workforce. All should be able to walk the walk.

- Teacher training should not incur tuition fees; teaching should move to a model like that in the NHS where the tuition fees of medical professionals are met by the state. This would make a two year professional route financially viable for students who have already incurred student debt in their undergraduate degree course.

A two year course might consist of the following elements:

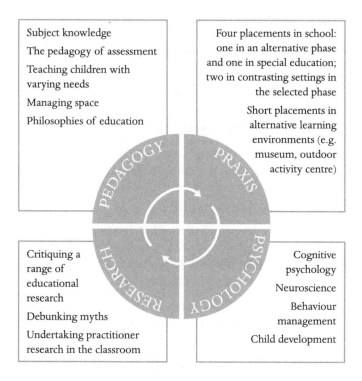

Subject knowledge

The pedagogy of assessment

Teaching children with varying needs

Managing space

Philosophies of education

Four placements in school: one in an alternative phase and one in special education; two in contrasting settings in the selected phase

Short placements in alternative learning environments (e.g. museum, outdoor activity centre)

Critiquing a range of educational research

Debunking myths

Undertaking practitioner research in the classroom

Cognitive psychology

Neuroscience

Behaviour management

Child development

PEDAGOGY

PRAXIS

RESEARCH

PSYCHOLOGY

Of course, all this costs. The question for government is whether or not our education system is worth it. And that depends on how much they believe in the power of education to impact on the economy and society as a whole. They say that it does. I would imagine that such expenditure might well be offset by the amount incurred by constantly retraining teachers because of high turnover, not to mention the significant costs to the wider economy of an unhappy, underachieving adult population.

Chapter 6

MOO COWS IN SHOWERS: CELEBRATING COMPLEXITY

Come, my friends,

'Tis not too late to seek a newer world.

Alfred, Lord Tennyson, *Ulysses* **(1842)**

When my youngest son was 2 years old he developed a strange fear. We frequently found him running from an imaginary tormenter screaming, 'Go way moo cow'. In the middle of the night, I would find him crouching in his bed, trembling and pointing to a corner of the room where he had cushions and a tent, and screaming, 'Moo cow in shower', over and over again. I knew he called his tent a 'shower', but there was no moo cow. I knew that he knew what a cow was because he could point to them and name them in his book. So what was he afraid of? There was no doubt that he was afraid of these offending moo cows, or at least of whatever it was behind the name he had given them. He was, of course, not seeing moo cows as we see or understand them. So, I watched him.

A pattern emerged. It seemed that whenever a shadow moved, he cried, 'Moo cow!' Walking in the woods, he noticed that the shadows of leaves from the trees were moving on his wellies. He jumped up, demanding to be carried, complaining, 'Moo cows on foots!' Did he mean shadows? Was it possible that he saw the dark patches on the cow's hide and thought they were shadows? Had he confused 'moo' with 'move'? I could not know but I was sure he was afraid of shadows. I named them for him. He called them 'moo shadow'. But he was still afraid. It was not for another three years that we were finally told by an optician that his eyes work independently of each other and that one side effect of this is terrifyingly real looking shadows. Suddenly, an amusing anecdote became a source of parental guilt. He was telling us that the world was different for him but we couldn't understand. As teachers, we do this every day to children. There are moo cows everywhere. And so we need to resist the temptation to reach for the simple – to create research models that seek to tell us 'what is' and 'what works' – and to seek instead to find ways of thinking and looking that accept the complexity of difference.

It is ironic, some might say hypocritical, to start this chapter with a medical story when it is my intention to outline for the remainder all the reasons why we must not be tempted to recreate a medical model of research in education. So be it. We should not use a medical model of research in education. Our children are not sicknesses and we are not, on the whole, looking for cures.

If I am a doctor, I do not expect to have to spend time working out how to help the healthy (though prevention is, indeed, better than cure). The people who come to see me are ill. There is something *wrong*, and if I am going to help them, I need to be sure of two things: (1) it won't make them worse and (2) it stands a good chance of making them better.

These aims can be measured. The patient is cured or not. In an ideal world, they go back to being what they were before they were ill. It is *never* the aim in education for children to return to what they were before you tried to educate them, and so our research can *never* carry the same level of certainty that medicine can. These difficulties seem to have bypassed the government who have appointed a doctor to tell them how to use research in education.[1] And here's the rub. Well, actually, another rub, because there are many rubs in this approach. (It is rubbish.) Even in medicine, there is a move away from the randomised controlled test approach. Or, at least, an acceptance of its limitations.

As genetic science evolves, there is an increasing realisation of the underlying complexity of human DNA. Although the number of genes is relatively few considering our differences (not that different to pigs, as it happens), beneath that porky similarity are millions of elements at a chemical level that make for mind-blowing complexity. In short, the more we try to simplify, the more intricate it becomes. As biological knowledge and technology develop, there is a move away from the collective, large scale testing of drugs towards a more individualised mapping of genes, with the ultimate goal of personalised care.[2] This development seeks to recognise the complexity while looking for some ways of finding common pathways. It is an interesting metaphor for education. Our children are individuals but we cannot cope

---

1 Ben Goldacre, Teachers! What Would Evidence Based Practice Look Like?, *Bad Science* (15 March 2013). Available at: http://www.badscience. net/2013/03/heres-my-paper-on-evidence-and-teaching-for-the-education-minister/.

2 See, for example, the 100,000 Genomes Project at: http://www. genomicsengland.co.uk/.

with teaching each one differently. As teachers, we need to find patterns in order to survive, but we must also reject all suggestions of silver bullets and simple solutions.

Just as our bodies are complex and individual, so are our minds. In addition to the many millions of synapses we have in our brains, there is an elaborate intra-relationship of proteins and particles which dwarf the number of brain cells and act in unknown ways across the wider body. In the words of neuroscientist Susan Greenfield:

The big and indeed unanswerable question now ... is what phenomenology can be matched up with this very physiological phenomenon of a neuronal assembly? ... The great question is still the causal, water-into-wine relationship of the physical brain and body with subjective mental events.[3]

Greenfield, like many other scientists, recognises that there is no certainty, only that 'this is what we know at this point'. It is this that Frank Furedi refers to as 'real science' – pioneering, uncertain, exploratory science that is accepting of unknowns (as opposed to 'scientism').[4] But we are compelled as a species, and particularly as an accountable profession, to reject the complex and to cling to the simple, ignoring almost wilfully the fact that there are no easy answers. As the physicist Richard Feynman said in explaining the structure of the atom, 'What is the outline? ... It is not, believe it or not, that every object has a line around it! There is no such line!' He went on to say, somewhat cheerfully, that 'it is not possible to predict what will happen in

3   Susan Greenfield, *You and Me: The Neuroscience of Identity* (London: Notting Hill Editions, 2011).

4   Frank Furedi, Keep the Scourge of Scientism Out of Schools, *Frank Furedi* (9 September 2013). Available at: http://www.frankfuredi.com/article/keep_the_scourge_of_scientism_out_of_schools.

any circumstance'.[5] I wish we could resurrect him and put him in charge of Ofsted. Neuroscientists use these uncertainties and complexities to warn against reductionist views of the brain, at the very same time that the education system is demanding that neuroscience gives them certain answers.

The reality is that classroom life is complex. Learning is not a linear process that can be tracked neatly on a graph, no matter how much we try to make it appear so. And making learning appear so means we become tempted to avoid engaging in the difficult in case it undermines the neatness of the line. When one is dealing with difference, there are only anomalies. Sameness can only be achieved by smoothing out complexity on such a large scale that individuals disappear. Hannah Arendt puts this problem across beautifully:

The laws of statistics are valid only where large numbers or long periods are involved, and acts or events can statistically appear only as deviations or fluctuations. ... Yet the meaningfulness of everyday relationships is disclosed not in everyday life but in rare deeds, just as the significance of a historical period shows itself only in the few events that illuminate it. The application of the law of large numbers and long periods to politics or history signifies nothing less than the willful obliteration of their very subject matter, and it is a hopeless enterprise to search for meaning in politics or significance in history when everything that is not everyday behavior or automatic trends has been ruled out as immaterial.[6]

5   Richard P. Feynman, *Six Easy Pieces: Fundamentals of Physics Explained* (London: Penguin, 1998), p. 35.

6   Hannah Arendt, *The Human Condition*, 2nd edn (Chicago, IL: University of Chicago Press, 1998 [1958]), pp. 42–43.

When we are trying to figure out what works in teaching, we try to simplify and clarify. The problems/outliers/differences become difficulties that we push to one side, but if you think differently – look for the moo cow – new ideas become apparent. We learn to realise that each child will respond to different approaches and we build a repertoire of techniques to help them. This takes time, experience and judgement. It is not easy, and it relies very much on building positive relationships and trust in classrooms.

Complex emotional elements are rarely considered in educational research yet they form crucial elements of learning. Hattie and Yates point out that children are highly attuned to the emotional authenticity of their teachers and are experts at spotting insincerity.[7] They point to the crucial importance of relationships in the classroom, and yet these elements are rarely measured in terms of education success, which, as we have seen, remains doggedly focused on exam results and testing, leading to a very narrow notion of accomplishment and progress.

Progress as a physical process built on relationships

In recent years, there has been a move towards questioning the idea that relevance and engagement matter in learning. I know. It sounds mad. But it ties in with the drive towards simplicity. For many teachers, the word engagement has been confused with entertainment and has been polluted by Ofsted grading criteria. But all brains must engage with content in order to remember. Engaging with content is

---

7   Hattie and Yates, *Visible Learning.*.

complex and emotional. And you can't always see it. Being entertained and having fun is not (necessarily) a sign of real engagement – that might better be thought of as investment or absorption. For this reason, points of engagement, like relationships, are hard to measure. Indeed, as many are now starting to point out, learning itself is hard to measure and it is certainly impossible to see in a single lesson.

Like engagement, relationships in the classroom are not about being 'nice' and being 'liked'. They are not about having fun all the time. They are rooted in the affective dimension and require watchfulness, humility and flexibility. They work on a complex interplay of actions, gestures, looks and words. A teacher who has great relationships notices things. The minutiae matter. And they matter because the brain is more complicated than some people like to think it is. For a start, physical and emotional processes are essential to our learning, even into adulthood.[8]

In the communities of neuroscience and cognitive psychology, there is an emerging consensus of wonder at the complex interplay between mind and body, which challenges the traditional model of cognition. This is a model that has evolved over centuries in a trajectory from Plato to Descartes to Freud. In this determinist model, there was thought to be a close relation between intelligence, conscious thought and human identity, with higher order thinking acting like a 'mini-me' of the conscious mind, collecting the information arriving from the senses and using logic and thought to organise, shape and present it in a clear-cut way. In this model, intuition and action are considered to be less 'intelligent' than rational thinking, so binaries are formed. This paradigm has permeated science for decades and has

---

8   Antonio Damasio, *Descartes' Error: Emotion, Reason and the Human Brain* (New York: J. P. Putman's Sons, 1994).

influenced education and research that has placed 'critical' and reasoned thinking as a pinnacle of intelligence.

Guy Claxton outlines these principles in an acronym – CLEVER:

Clear-cut *(not vague)*

Logical *(dispassionate)*

Explicit *(well justified and not heart-felt)*

Verbal *(not manifest in gesture or expression)*

Explanatory *(not manifest in action or perception)*

Rapid *(requiring neither patience nor contemplation)*[9]

Yet there is a series of studies which show a complex and interrelated system of knowing in which the physical, emotional and intellectual are mutually dependent and variably expressed, leading many, including Claxton, to suggest that:

The idea popularly attributed to Jean Paiget and widely believed in education, that we 'grow out of' our reliance on the concrete and the sensorimotor and that once we achieve 'formal operations' we can happily kick away the ladder of physical experience that helped us to get there, turns out to be highly questionable. Bodies are a whole lot more than vehicles for getting minds to classrooms and they may deserve a greater and more sophisticated role in education than merely 'letting off steam' on the sports field.[10]

9 Guy Claxton, Turning Thinking On Its Head: How Bodies Make Up Their Minds, *Thinking Skills and Creativity* 7(2) (2012): 78–84.

10 Claxton, Turning Thinking On Its Head, p. 81.

In traditional modes of teaching, the body can be seen at best as an irrelevance, at worst a distraction. In fact, the body can tell us a great deal about what a child knows or is in the process of knowing. There are high levels of activity occurring in what sometimes feel like moments of stillness and silence.

We know from recent developments in neuroscience that many 'conversations' take place in this space and they are conversations that can powerfully shape the mood of the participants. Indeed, it is almost impossible to separate the emotional, motor and higher order thinking processes, and where it is possible there is damage to the brain.[11] Moreover, the body's motor system reacts to metaphor and imagination as quickly and effectively as it does to reality. Claxton notes that, unsurprisingly, when we hear a sentence such as, 'Bill caught the cricket ball', our hand primes itself to catch a ball. He goes on to cite studies from Masson, Bub and Newton-Taylor[12] and Glenberg et al.[13] in which similar physiological responses occur in sentences such as, 'Anna had forgotten her Blackberry' (listeners primed their motor cortex to make small pressing motions with their thumbs), and even in more abstract modes such as, 'Judith delegated the responsibility to Sheena', where the motor cortex indicated a gesture of giving – open palm out. While we linguistically accept that metaphors such as 'kicking habits' or 'pushing up daisies' mean other things, our brains still react literally to them, priming our legs and hands to kick and push. Do the words 'can't' and 'can' have a similar impact?

----

11 Damasio, *Descartes' Error*.

12 Michael Masson, Daniel Bub and Meaghan Newton-Taylor, Language-Based Access to Gestural Components of Conceptual Knowledge, *Quarterly Journal of Experimental Psychology* 61(6) (2008): 869–882.

13 Arthur Glenberg, Marc Sato, Luigi Cattaneo, Lucia Riggio, Daniele Palumbo and Giovanni Buccino, Processing Abstract Language Modulates Motor System Activity, *Quarterly Journal of Experimental Psychology* 61(6) (2008): 1–15.

In an observation, a senior leader commented that it was good that I was not afraid of silence and would wait. I wanted to say that there was no silence, there is talk all the time; it's just gestural talk, waiting for words to catch up. Susan Goldin-Meadow and Susan Wagner point out that gestures are the essence of explanation, and that children will frequently convey meanings and understandings much richer than their words suggest through gesture.[14] They argue that paralinguistic features of communication are often more daring and creative than children are willing to express in words or writing. We dance our language – sometimes imperceptibly, sometimes clearly.

I knew it but I didn't know I knew it when I was teaching a Year 9 class and trying to get them to identify metaphor. I ask whether they can tell me what a metaphor is. One boy is bobbing, hand in the air, but when he tries to say it, he falters.

'I thought I knew, it's … No, I can't explain it.'

Normally I would move on, but I've just read about embodied cognition and so I look at the boy's hands.

'Look at your hands – what are they trying to tell you?' He looks. His hands are making a curved shape – a bit like the shape men make of women, a bit like a vase. I'm not sure which, but his hands are moving in this shape without him knowing.

'Oh, it's like a vase … a vessel … Is a metaphor a vessel – like a container for a meaning? Oh, I can't say it!'

'You did – you found a metaphor for a metaphor.'

---

14 Susan Goldin-Meadow and Susan Wagner, How Our Hands Help Us Learn, *Trends in Cognitive Science* 9(5) (2005): 234–241.

If we are really going to help children to make progress, we need to think about it completely differently. Progress is not about putting numbers into spreadsheets. It is about seizing on small but significant moments of opportunity. Clues. Being open to possibility. Being positive.

Too often, teachers fail to see those small moments of something that can so easily be lost. We fail to capitalise on clues – to probe a hesitant speaker, to see an embodied explanation. We let them go and they become lost in the frustration of knowing that they almost knew but not quite. We need to capitalise on these moments – to recognise and pull them out – in order to truly understand what it is that children know and are on the verge of understanding. In terms of educational research, we need to look beyond what seems to work in securing test results to exploring instead what it is that makes a human being work. How does the brain learn? We need to understand that cognitive psychologists and scientists tend to look at narrow areas of expertise – gesture *or* working memory *or* speech – but rarely bring those areas together. We need to do that for ourselves, to connect and to find what works for us. This is a wholly more demanding task but it is what reality demands.

Implications for your classroom

♦ Susan Goldin-Meadow's research shows that teachers who gesture well impact more highly on children's understanding of concepts – children are highly attuned to your movements so make sure they can see you.

- She also found that children tend to mime their under-standing with their hands before their knowledge translates into words. Building in opportunities for children to reflect their learning through movement may help in this process – certainly, teachers should watch carefully children's movements.

- Don't be afraid of 'the void' – the awkward silence and stillness that sometimes follows the setting of a task. Children need time to think and if you jump in too quickly, you remove the need to think.

- Never fake your data. Argue the case that reporting should move beyond numbers and scores so that parents and children have a clear idea of what is known and what needs to be developed.

- Accept that learning doesn't move in straight lines.

- Remember that behind every set of data lies a story and that there are multiple interpretations of each set of figures. Much as we would like to disbelieve it, the truth is always a set of shifting sands.

- Develop a 'triple A' pedagogy, recognising that activity, articulacy and autonomy are precursors to effective writing.

Chapter 7

(R)EVOLUTION: PEDAGOGICAL ACTIVISM

I hope our wisdom will grow with our power, and teach us,
that the less we use our power, the greater it will be.

Thomas Jefferson (1815)

There have been no darker times in education in my memory and I have taught for over twenty years. The removal of a single controversial figure cannot make a dent in a global ideology that is pervasive across continents. Systematic attacks on childhood, on teachers, on academics and on parents have led to hopelessness and despondency. This is reflected in the large numbers of teachers leaving the profession – around 40–50% in the first five years[1] – a pattern consistent in GERM nations such as the US, UK and Australia. It is not so simple as to point to workload in understanding this phenomenon. Teaching is emotional work. Relationships are essential to success and yet it is this aspect of the work that suffers the most when people are tired and stressed. Addressing teacher burn out is critical if we are to retain the best in the profession.

---

1   Andrew McMillen, School's Out Early for Overworked and Undersupported Young Teachers, *The Guardian* (6 August 2013). Available at: http://www.theguardian.com/education/2013/aug/06/teachers-leave-profession-early.

Even more worrying are the soaring mental health problems in our young – as many as one in ten children suffer from mental health issues.[2] And we should heed the suicide rate in South Korea among schoolchildren – the highest in the world and which even their government puts down in part to 'exam stress' – before we try to emulate their education system. It is difficult to hope in such times but we must. Hope gives impetus for action and actions make marks. But what can we learn from current failures? Where might future hopes lie?

Hope is not a market commodity

I briefly mentioned Pasi Sahlberg's analysis of OECD data in Chapter 3 in which he calls attention to a critical point of similarity in the nations deemed to be falling in the tables.[3] Putting all the statistical uncertainties surrounding those tests aside, one striking feature of them is that they indicate a failure of the Global Education Reform Movement. This movement is built on the principle that market forces can act as a driver for improvement in education, yet it is not the case that where these policies are in place (characterised by free/charter schools, high levels of punitive accountability and a dependency on high stakes testing) that any improvement occurs. In fact, the opposite seems to be true. According to Sahlberg, there is little doubt that the market driven policies advocated in the US, Britain, Sweden and

----

2   See Mental Health Foundation: http://www.mentalhealth.org.uk/help-information/mental-health-a-z/C/children-young-people/.

3   Pasi Sahlberg, The PISA 2012 Scores Show the Failure of 'Market Based' Education Reform, *The Guardian* (8 December 2013). Available at: http://www.theguardian.com/commentisfree/2013/dec/08/pisa-education-test-scores-meaning.

other countries in recent times have not yielded the kinds of improvements that were craved. As Melissa Benn points out, it is now clear that state schools, coming from the same starting point, are outperforming academies in terms of improvement.[4] Moreover, she states that in the free (or charter) school movement in the US, it is becoming apparent that the zero-tolerance behaviour policies advocated by the much acclaimed KIPP (Knowledge Is Power Program) chain have led to a disproportionate number of children from ethnic minorities and those with special educational needs being excluded. When we consider that the rhetoric driving the market driven approach claimed that it would reduce social inequality and increase social mobility, these facts raise serious concerns. It is increasingly clear that market driven educational policies are failing. Where successes emerge (leaving aside nations reliant on inhumane practices), they lie in equality and in a belief that all can succeed. No Child Left Behind as a reality, not a slogan.

Nevertheless, it is always necessary to hope and to believe that things will get better. As the old saying goes, the darkest hour is just before dawn. What might dawn bring?

A manifesto for a pedagogical activist

While writing this book, I have hoped. I have hoped that you, my reader (or hopefully more than one of you), will have considered your own part to be played in solving the problems we have in education. That you may have considered what might be done to work outside the system even

---

4   Melissa Benn and Fiona Millar, Why Market Driven Education has Failed. Speech delivered at the *Sunday Times* Festival of Education, Wellington College, Berkshire, 20–21 June 2014.

while within it. I have hoped that we might, regardless of our differences in philosophy or approach, agree that it is important for children to find joy in knowledge and learning and to want that they retain that learning throughout their adult lives. I have hoped that we might all agree that teaching is far too important not to make it worth investing in an equable system of excellence in training new generations of teachers, regardless of cost. I have hoped that, in spite of what differences of opinion we might have about pedagogy, we all recognise that childhood is precious and that every child has the right to learn in a safe, trusting and supportive environment. I have hoped that we can come together and change the world. Make a dent in the universe, as Steve Jobs said.

We can do this in two ways: on a national stage or on our personal stage. There are some of us who tub-thump and shout in blogs, tweets, letters and meetings – political activists. And there are others who challenge injustice, build hope and resist nonsense in their classrooms – pedagogical activists. I believe that it is pedagogical activism that will prove to be the butterfly wing of change.

What if every teacher took an oath to do the following:

- ◆ I refuse to compete with my colleagues but seek instead to collaborate.

- ◆ I refuse to see exam results as the sole point of my role – I can see beyond the horizon of tests.

- ◆ I value children's happiness as much as their academic success.

- ◆ I understand the importance of relationships, of smiling, of being there for the children I teach.

♦ I know that children need hope, so I will offer stories of resilience and success and refuse to scaremonger.

♦ I refuse to give up on a child, even when I recognise that others might be better placed to help them.

♦ I refuse to despair – I own my classroom and will teach as I see fit.

♦ I recognise that trust is built by sharing my own vulnerabilities as well as accepting those of others.

♦ I know that no matter how tired I am, I need to read, to keep up to date with new developments in education and to keep on networking.

♦ I'll never stop questioning and sharing those questions with children.

If these actions were taken, then children would see school differently. They would see that here is a place where they are seen as more than a set of results. A place where the world becomes interesting for them. A place where the future is bursting with possibility. A place where they are loved and can learn to love. All this as well as a place where they can pass exams or (she prays) succeed in whatever qualification system replaces exams.

Hope is not built on grand gestures or sudden actions, but in small, accumulative (r)evolutionary practices. It springs from the cracks between our questions and solutions. Rather than becoming despondent at our smallness, we should use our size to our advantage. We're on the ground, interacting with children every single day. We matter.

We need this teachers' manifesto – one in which we make a pledge to be brave, to be imagineers of learning (to borrow from Hywel Roberts again), to be kind, to be constructors and designers of hope. Because without these things, we are the messengers of whichever master we are forced to serve. We are inconstant and inconsistent. We are lost.

Manage your image

We need to gather, to create networks and to share our stories of resilience and resistance. We need to use social networking to create the 'disruptive liberation' model of technology that Charles Leadbeater sees as the potentiality of technology to build communities with shared goals.[5] We need to be attentive and agentive in recognising the needs of the children we teach and be vocal about any abuses they are suffering under our particularly punitive current model of education. We need to seize every moment we can to talk to parents about the system – not only telling them that their child is on target for a certain grade but also educating them about how a child's brain works and what they can do to build growth and positivity. We should start running CPD for parents.

What would this look like? Imagine a series of courses or meetings that had titles like this instead of, 'Helping your child with phonics':

+ How your child's brain works.

+ Why exams are a tiny part of what is important to your child's future.

+ Building a growth mindset in your child.

+ What would a perfect school look like (you tell us).

5   Charles Leadbeater, Technology in Education: The Past, Present and Future. Speech delivered at the *Sunday Times* Festival of Education, Wellington College, Berkshire, 21–22 June 2013.

♦ The reality behind the headlines.

♦ Why we're not as bad as you think we are.

Okay, you might want to play with those a little, but if parents knew the stories behind the headlines, if they understood how children learn, if they could see and know what it's like to teach a class, how would that impact on the failure narratives in the media?

It's a scary thing, but I sometimes invite parents into 'open classes', and it does more for our relationship than a hundred written reports, warts and all. What if all schools did this? What if *you* did this?

We also need to think about how we can build new assessment models, even if they must sit alongside the old ones for now. For example, in our school we set aside an hour for Year 7 and 8 pupils, the Pupil Driven Review, in which a parent sits with a teacher, their child and three peers, listening to a self-assessment presentation by their child, a peer review by their classmates, a teacher review by their teacher and, finally, a session in which targets are set.[6] This is humanising assessment and there's not a grade in sight. It follows on from the extended project – a 2,000 word essay in response to a philosophical question that all pupils answer, with questions like, 'Is life a postcode lottery?', 'Is poverty inevitable?' and 'Is the world a fair place?' No one can argue that there is not rigour in this process. But there are no grades. Instead, there are meaningful conversations about learning, and the peer reporting is an extremely powerful part of that process. The peers follow and report on the child – one on progress, one on skills and one on behaviour

---

6 Debra Kidd, Assessment As An Act of Love, *Teaching Times* (1 May 2009). Available to purchase at: http://www.teachingtimes.com/kb/70/assessment-for-learning.htm.

and attitude. Believe me, there is more weight behind a child saying, 'I've stopped sitting next to you because you talk a lot and I can't concentrate – you need to think about how your chatting affects other people,' as happened in one session, than there is in a teacher telling a parent that their child is a bit chatty. Hearing it from a peer has a significant impact on both children and parents. In addition, it is clear that seeing their child become a little more thoughtful about the world has a significant impact on parents too. Consider this from the parent of a Year 8 child:

The Pupil Driven Review on poverty last year had a massive impact on her emotionally; made her think about becoming an engineer to drill water bores ... and this year she has really questioned her own ability to forgive, and under what circumstance.

Many thanks for your compassion.

How often do we hear parents' views on their child's shifting perceptions of the world? What contributions do we make to those perceptions? We may not be able to end our reliance on exams, and many won't want to, but we can certainly foster more holistic models of assessment in our own classrooms and schools.

A final thought

Our evolution as teachers requires that we start our journey towards a new education by changing ourselves first. By reframing our concept of what is possible – becoming Mobius-like. We need to work within a system. We are accountable. But we can simultaneously be within and without, looking in and out. We can be school friendly and child friendly – like the Mobius strip being inner and outer. We can reject market forces – we don't have to buy their stuff. We can reject the nay-sayers by remaining sceptical of their failure narratives. We can hope and share hopefulness. We are kings of our own classrooms and, most of the time, no one else is looking. Be yourself and do what you know is right. Keep connected – use social media, attend the many grassroots conferences and TeachMeets taking place across the country by teachers for teachers, read and share your reading, set up a drop-in centre in your classroom for colleagues, parents and pupils to build a 'free from fear' culture of collaboration. By doing these things, we'll create the oscillations for change. We'll give children the education they deserve. We'll be the teacher we deserve to be.

Bibliography

Allen, Rebecca and Jay Allnutt (2013). Matched Panel Data Estimates of the Impact of TeachFirst on School and Departmental Performance. Department of Quantitative Social Science Working Paper No. 13-11. Available at: http://repec.ioe.ac.uk/REPEc/pdf/qsswp1311.pdf.

Altshuler, Sandra J. and Tresa Schmautz (2005). No Hispanic Student Left Behind: The Consequence of 'High Stakes' Testing, *Children and Schools: A Journal of the National Association of Social Workers* 28(1): 5–14.

Arendt, Hannah (1998 [1958]). *The Human Condition*, 2nd edn (Chicago, IL: University of Chicago Press).

Arya, Diana and Andrew Maul (2012). The Role of the Scientific Discovery Narrative in Middle School Science Education: An Experimental Study, *Journal of Educational Psychology* 104(4): 1022–1032.

Baird, Jo-Anne, Ayesha Ahmed, Therese Hopfenbeck, Carol Brown and Victoria Elliot (2013). *Research Evidence Relating to Proposals for Reform of the GCSE*. Oxford University Centre for Educational Assessment Report OUCEA/13/1. Available at: http://oucea.education.ox.ac.uk/wordpress/wp-content/uploads/2013/04/WCQ-report-final.pdf.

Ball, Stephen (2012). *The Education Debate*, 2nd edn (Bristol: Policy Press).

Barber, Michael and Mona Mourshed (2007). *How the World's Best-Performing Schools Come Out On Top* (New York: McKinsey & Co.) Available at: http://mckinseyonsociety.com/downloads/reports/Education/Worlds_School_Systems_Final.pdf.

Baumann, Claudia Erni and Roman Boutellier (2012). Physical Activity: The Basis of Learning and Creativity. Paper presented at the Future of Education Conference, Florence, Italy, 7–8 June. Available at: http://conference.pixelonline.net/edu_future/common/download/Paper_pdf/ITL59-Baumann.pdf.

Benn, Melissa and Fiona Millar (2014). Why Market Driven Education has Failed. Speech delivered at the *Sunday Times* Festival of Education, Wellington College, Berkshire, 20–21 June.

Black, Paul and Dylan Wiliam (1998). *Inside the Black Box: Raising Standards Through Classroom Assessment* (London: School of Education, King's College).

Boffey, Daniel and Warwick Mansell (2014). Revealed: Gove's Bid to Limit Fallout from Failing Free Schools, *The Observer* (6 April). Available at: http://www.theguardian.com/education/2014/apr/06/michael-gove-failing-free-schools.

Brighouse, Tim (2009). All I Want for Education, *The Guardian* (2 January). Available at: http://www.theguardian.com/education/2009/jan/02/tim-brighouse-wishlist.

Burns, Judith (2013). Ofsted Methods May Not Be Valid, Says Senior Academic, *BBC News* (13 September). Available at: http://www.bbc.co.uk/news/education-24079951.

Charette, Robert (2010). London Stock Exchange New Trading Platform 'Twice as Fast' as Rivals, *IEEE Spectrum* (20 October). Available at: http://spectrum.ieee.org/riskfactor/computing/it/london-stock-exchange-new-trading-platform-twice-as-fast-as-rivals.

Claxton, Guy (2012). Turning Thinking On Its Head: How Bodies Make Up Their Minds, *Thinking Skills and Creativity* 7(2): 78–84.

Christodoulou, Daisy (2014a). *Seven Myths About Education* (Abingdon: Routledge/Curriculum Centre).

Christodoulou, Daisy (2014b). Why National Curriculum Levels Need Replacing, *The Wing to Heaven* (3 April). Available at: http://thewingtoheaven.wordpress.com/2014/04/03/why-national-curriculum-levels-need-replacing/.

Cladingbowl, Michael (2014). *Why I Want to Try Inspecting Without Grading Teaching in Each Individual Lesson* (4 June). Ref: 140101. Available at: http://www.ofsted.gov.uk/resources/why-i-want-try-inspecting-without-grading-teaching-each-individual-lesson.

Coe, Robert (2013a). Improving Education: A Triumph of Hope Over Experience. Inaugural lecture, Centre for Evaluation and Monitoring, Durham University. Available at: http://www.cem.org/attachments/publications/ImprovingEducation2013.pdf.

Coe, Robert (2013b). Practice and Research in Education: How Can We Make Both Better, and Better Aligned? Paper presented at researchED Midlands, June. Video available at: http://www.researched2013.co.uk/professor-robert-coe-at-researched-2013/.

Coughlan, Sean (2014). England's Schools Succeed in Problem-Solving Test, *BBC News* (1 April). Available at: http://www.bbc.co.uk/news/education-26823184.

Damasio, Antonio (1994). *Descartes' Error: Emotion, Reason and the Human Brain* (New York: J. P. Putman's Sons).

Deleuze, Gilles (1992). Postscript on the Control Societies, *October* 59 (Winter): 3–7.

Department for Work and Pensions (2012). *Measuring Child Poverty: A Consultation of Better Measures of Child Poverty* (November). Cm. 8483 (London: The Stationery Office). Available at: https://www.gov.uk/government/uploads/system/uploads/attachment_data/file/228829/8483.pdf.

Gilles, Deleuze (1990 [1969]). *The Logic of Sense*, tr. Mark Lester with Charles Stivale, ed. Constantin V. Boundas (New York: Colombia University Press).

Dunlosky, John, Katherine Rawson, Elizabeth Marsh, Mitchell Nathan and Daniel Willingham (2013). Improving Students' Learning with Effective Learning Techniques: Promising Directions from Cognitive and Educational Psychology, *Psychological Science in the Public Interest* 14 (January): 4–58.

Edelman, Gerald M. (1982). *The Mindful Brain: Cortical Organization and the Group-Selective Theory of Higher Brain Function* (Cambridge, MA: MIT Press).

Education Select Committee (2012). The Responsibilities of the Secretary of State for Education, HC 1786-i, 2010–2012 (31 January). Available at: http://www.publications.parliament.uk/pa/cm201012/cmselect/cmeduc/uc1786-i/uc178601.htm.

Feynman, Richard P. (1998). *Six Easy Pieces: Fundamentals of Physics Explained* (London: Penguin).

Furedi, Frank (2013). Keep the Scourge of Scientism Out of Schools, *Frank Furedi* (9 September). Available at: http://www.frankfuredi.com/article/keep_the_scourge_of_scientism_out_of_schools.

Garner, Richard (2013). 'Sheer Scale of Prescription' Under Michael Gove's Planned New Curriculum Will Turn Pupils Off Science Lessons, Warn Business Leaders, *The Independent* (16 April). Available at: http://www.independent.co.uk/news/business/news/sheer-scale-of-prescription-under-michael-goves-planned-new-curriculum-will-turn-pupils-off-science-lessons-warn-business-leaders-8575614.html.

Gibb, Nick (2014). Teaching Unions Aren't the Problem – Universities Are, *The Guardian* (23 April). Available at: http://www.theguardian.com/commentisfree/2014/apr/23/teaching-unions-arent-problem-universities-schools-minister?CMP=twt_gu#start-of-comments.

Gladwell, Malcolm (2008). *Outliers: The Story of Success* (New York: Little, Brown and Co.).

Glenberg, Arthur, Marc Sato, Luigi Cattaneo, Lucia Riggio, Daniele Palumbo and Giovanni Buccino (2008). Processing Abstract Language Modulates Motor System Activity, *Quarterly Journal of Experimental Psychology* 61(6): 1–15.

Goldacre, Ben (2013a). *Building Evidence into Education* (London: Department for Education). Available at: http://media.education.gov.uk/assets/files/pdf/b/ben%20goldacre%20paper.pdf.

Goldacre, Ben (2013b).Teachers! What Would Evidence Based Practice Look Like?, *Bad Science* (15 March). Available at: http://www.badscience.net/2013/03/heres-my-paper-on-evidence-and-teaching-for-the-education-minister/.

Goldin-Meadow, Susan and Susan Wagner (2005). How Our Hands Help Us Learn, *Trends in Cognitive Science* 9(5): 234–241.

Gore, Al (2013). *Future: Six Drivers of Global Change* (New York: Random House).

Gove, Michael (2013). I Refuse to Surrender to the Marxist Teachers Hell-Bent on Destroying Our Schools, *Daily Mail* (23 March). Available at: http://www.dailymail.co.uk/debate/article-2298146/I-refuse-surrender-Marxist-teachers-hell-bent-destroying-schools-Education-Secretary-berates-new-enemies-promise-opposing-plans.html.

Hanushek, Eric and Ludger Woessmann (2010). *The High Cost of Low Educational Performance: The Long-Run Economic Impact of Improving PISA Outcomes* (Paris: OECD Programme for International Student Assessment). Available at: http://www.oecd.org/pisa/44417824.pdf.

Hattie, John (2009). *Visible Learning: A Synthesis of Over 800 Meta-Analyses Relating to Achievement* (London: Routledge).

Hattie, John and Greg Yates (2013). *Visible Learning and the Science of How We Learn* (Abingdon: Routledge).

Headteachers' Roundtable (2013). Qualifications Framework Proposal (May). Available at: http://headteachersroundtable.files.wordpress.com/2013/05/the-headteachers-roundtable-qualifications-framework-proposal-final.pdf.

Heavey, Susan (2013). Number of Working Poor Families Grows As Wealth Gap Widens, *Reuters* (15 January). Available at: http://www.reuters.com/article/2013/01/15/us-usa-economy-workingpoor-idUSBRE90E05520130115.

Hirsch, E. D. (2006) *The Knowledge Deficit: Closing the Shocking Education Gap for American Children* (New York: Houghton Mifflin).

Ho, Andrew and Thomas Kane (2013). *The Reliability of Classroom Observations by School Personnel* (Seattle, WA: Bill & Melinda Gates Foundation). Available at: http://www.metproject.org/downloads/MET_Reliability_of_Classroom_Observations_Research_Paper.pdf.

House of Commons Education Committee (2012). *Great Teachers: Attracting, Training and Retaining the Best. Ninth Report on Session 2010–12.* Ref: HC 1515-II (London: The Stationery Office). Available at: http://www.publications.parliament.uk/pa/cm201012/cmselect/cmeduc/1515/1515ii.htm.

House of Commons Education Committee (2013). *Careers Guidance for Young People: The Impact of the New Duty on Schools. Seventh Report of Session 2012–13.* Ref: HC 632 (London: The Stationery Office). Available at: http://www.publications.parliament.uk/pa/cm201213/cmselect/cmeduc/632/632.pdf.

Katsiyannis, Antonis, Dalun Zhang, Joseph B. Ryan and Julie Jones (2007). High-Stakes Testing and Students with Disabilities: Challenges and Promises, *Journal of Disability Policy Studies* 18(3): 160–167.

Kidd, Debra (2009). Assessment As An Act of Love, *Teaching Times* (1 May). Available to purchase at: http://www.teachingtimes.com/kb/70/assessment-for-learning.htm.

Leadbeater, Charles (2013). Technology in Education: The Past, Present and Future. Speech delivered at the *Sunday Times* Festival of Education, Wellington College, Berkshire, 21–22 June.

Lencioni, Patrick (2002). *The Five Dysfunctions of a Team: A Leadership Fable* (Garden City, NY: Wiley).

Levitt, Steven and Stephen Dubner (2005). *Freakonomics: A Rogue Economist Explores the Hidden Side of Everything* (New York: William Morrow).

Lowrey, Annie (2013). Switzerland's Proposal to Pay People for Being Alive, *New York Times* (12 November). Available at: http://mobile.nytimes.com/2013/11/17/magazine/switzerlands-proposal-to-pay-people-for-being-alive.html.

McMillen, Andrew (2013). School's Out Early for Overworked and Undersupported Young Teachers, *The Guardian* (6 August). Available at: http://www.theguardian.com/education/2013/aug/06/teachers-leave-profession-early.

Mansell, Warwick (2014). Free Schools Fail Ofsted Inspections at a Much Higher Rate Than State Schools, *The Guardian* (29 April). Available at: http://www.theguardian.com/education/2014/apr/29/free-schools-ofsted-failure-rate-higher-state.

Masson, Micahel, Daniel Bub and Meaghan Newton-Taylor (2008). Language-Based Access to Gestural Components of Conceptual Knowledge, *Quarterly Journal of Experimental Psychology* 61(6): 869–882.

Millar, Fiona (2013). Who Is Really Behind Michael Gove's Big Education Ideas?, *The Guardian* (3 December). Available at: http://www.theguardian.com/education/2013/dec/03/michael-gove-education-dominic-cummings-policies-oxbridge.

Ofsted (2011). *The Annual Report of Her Majesty's Chief Inspector of Education, Children's Services and Skills* 2010/11. Ref: HC 1633 (London: The Stationery Office). Available at: https://www.gov.uk/government/uploads/system/uploads/attachment_data/file/247177/1633.pdf.

Park, James (2013). *Detoxifying School Accountability* (London: Demos). Available at: http://www.demos.co.uk/files/Detoxifying_School_Accountability__web.pdf?1367602207.

Peacock, Alison (2013). *Towards a Royal College of Teaching: Raising the Status of the Profession* (London: Royal College of Surgeons of England).

Peal, Robert (2014). *Progressively Worse: The Burden of Bad Ideas in British Schools* (London: Civitas).

Pink, Daniel (2009). *Drive: The Surprising Truth About What Motivates Us* (New York: Riverhead).

Robertson, Susan L. (2008). *'Remaking the World': Neo-Liberalism and the Transformation of Education and Teachers' Labour* (Bristol: Centre for Globalisation, Education and Societies, University of Bristol). Available at: http://www.bris.ac.uk/education/people/academicStaff/edslr/publications/17slr.

Roberts, Hywel (2012). *Oops! Helping Children Learn Accidentally* (Carmarthen: Independent Thinking Press).

Roy, Kaustuv (2003). *Teachers in Nomadic Spaces: Deleuze and Curriculum* (New York: Peter Lang). Available at: http://2020research.files.wordpress.com/2011/06/roy-deleuze-teachers-in-nomadic-spaces.pdf.

Ruiz-Primo, Maria, Richard J. Shavelson, Laura Hamilton and Steve Klein (2002). On the Evaluation of Systemic Science Education Reform: Searching for Instructional Sensitivity, *Journal of Research in Science Teaching* 39(5): 369–393.

Sahlberg, Pasi (2010). Rethinking Accountability in a Knowledge Society, *Journal of Educational Change* 11: 45–61. Available at: http://pasisahlberg.com/wp-content/uploads/2013/01/Rethinking-accountability-JEC-2010.pdf.

Sahlberg, Pasi (2012). Four Questions About Education in Finland, *Pasi Sahlberg Blog* (9 April). Available at: http://pasisahlberg.com/four-questions-about-education-in-finland/.

Sahlberg, Pasi (2013). The PISA 2012 Scores Show the Failure of 'Market Based' Education Reform, *The Guardian* (8 December). Available at: http://www.theguardian.com/commentisfree/2013/dec/08/pisa-education-test-scores-meaning.

Seligman, Martin (1991). *Learned Optimism: How to Change Your Mind and Your Life* (New York: Knopf).

Seligman, Martin (2002). *Authentic Happiness: Using the New Positive Psychology to Realise Your Potential for Lasting Fulfilment* (New York: Free Press).

Sherrington, Tom (2014). Meeting Ofsted: The Game Has Changed, *Headguruteacher* (20 February). Available at: http://headguruteacher. com/2014/02/20/meeting-ofsted/.

Social Mobility and Child Poverty Commission (2013). *State of the Nation 2013: Social Mobility and Child Poverty in Great Britain* (London: The Stationery Office). Available at: https://www.gov.uk/government/ uploads/system/uploads/attachment_data/file/292231/ State_of_the_Nation_2013.pdf.

Sparrow, Stephanie (2008). Classroom Craftsman, *Make the Grade* (Spring): 25–27. Available at: http://www.dylanwiliam.org/ Dylan_Wiliams_website/Bios_files/CIEA%20interview.pdf.

Strauss, Valerie (2014). Kindergarten Show Canceled So Kids Can Keep Studying to Become 'College and Career Ready.' Really. *Washington Post* (26 April). Available at: http://www.washingtonpost.com/blogs/ answer-sheet/wp/2014/04/26/kindergarten-show-canceled-so-kids-can-keep-working-to-become-college-and-career-ready-really/.

Sutton Trust and Education Endowment Foundation (2013). *Teaching and Learning Toolkit* (London: Education Endowment Foundation). Available at: http://educationendowmentfoundation.org.uk/uploads/ toolkit/Teaching_and_Learning_Toolkit_%28Spring_2013%29.pdf.

Swaffield, Sue (2009). The Misrepresentation of Assessment for Learning and the Woeful Waste of a Wonderful Opportunity. Paper presented at the Association for Achievement and Improvement through Assessment National Conference, Bournemouth, 16–18 December. Available at: http://cdn.aaia.org.uk/content/uploads/2010/07/ The-Misrepresentation-of-Assessment-for-Learning1.pdf.

Sylwester, Robert (1994). How Emotions Affect Learning, *Educational Leadership* 52(2): 60–65. Available at: http://www.ascd.org/publications/ educational-leadership/oct94/vol52/num02/How-Emotions-Affect-Learning.aspx.

TeachFirst (2013), *Annual Review 2012/13* (London: TeachFirst). Available at: http://www.teachfirst.org.uk/sites/default/files/ar/pdf/Annual%20 Review%202013%20web.pdf.

Thomas, Gerran (1999). Standards and School Inspection: The Rhetoric and the Reality, in Cedric Cullingford (ed.), *An Inspector Calls: Ofsted and Its Effect on School Standards* (London: Kogan Page), pp. 135–148.

Torrance, Harry (2007). Assessment As Learning? How the Use of Explicit Learning Objectives, Assessment Criteria and Feedback in Post-Secondary Education and Training Can Come to Dominate Learning, *Assessment in Education* 14(3): 281–294. Available at: http://www.academia.edu/3488529/Assessment_as_learning_How_the_use_of_explicit_learning_objectives_assessment_criteria_and_feedback_in_post-secondary_education_and_training_can_come_to_dominate_learning/.

Truss, Elizabeth (2014). Elizabeth Truss Speaks About Improving Teaching. Speech delivered at Reform, London, 10 April. Available at: https://www.gov.uk/government/speeches/elizabeth-truss-speaks-about-improving-teaching.

Ward, Helen (2012). Assessment for Learning Has Fallen Prey to Gimmicks, Says Critic, *TES* (15 July). Available at: http://www.tes.co.uk/article.aspx?storycode=6003863.

Waters, Mick (2013). *Thinking Allowed on Schooling* (Carmarthen, Independent Thinking Press).

Wiliam, Dylan (2010). An Integrative Summary of the Research Literature and Implications for a New Theory of Formative Assessment, in Heidi L. Andrade and Gregory J. Cizek (eds.), *Handbook of Formative Assessment* (New York and Abingdon: Routledge), pp. 18–40.

Wilkinson, Richard and Kate Pickett (2010). *The Spirit Level: Why Equality is Better for Everyone* (London: Penguin).

Williams, James (2011). *Gilles Deleuze's Philosophy of Time: A Critical Introduction and Guide* (Edinburgh: Edinburgh University Press).

Williams, Zoe (2014). George Lakoff: 'Conservatives Don't Follow the Polls, They Want to Change Them … Liberals Do Everything Wrong', *The Guardian* (1 February). Available at: http://www.theguardian.com/books/2014/feb/01/george-lakoff-interview.

Willingham, Daniel (2013). How to Make Edu-Blogging Less Boring, *Daniel Willingham* (30 July). Available at: http://www.danielwillingham.com/1/post/2013/07/how-to-make-edu-blogging-less-boring.html.

Wilmut, John, Robert Wood, and Roger Murphy (1996). A Review of Research Into the Reliability of Examinations. Discussion paper prepared for the School Curriculum and Assessment Authority, University of Nottingham. Available at: http://www.nottingham.ac.uk/education/centres/cdell/pdf-reportsrelexam/relexam.pdf.

Wood, Phil and Wasyl Cajkler (2013). Beyond Communities of Practice: Investigating and Developing the Professional Learning of Trainee Teachers Through Lesson Study. Research report for the Society for Educational Studies. Available at: http://www.soc-for-ed-studies.org.uk/documents/smallgrants/finalReports/wood-and-cajkler.pdf.

Wylie, Caroline and Dylan Wiliam (2006), Analyzing Diagnostic Items: What Makes a Student Response Interpretable? Paper presented at the annual meeting of the National Council on Measurement in Education, Chicago, IL, April. Available at: http://www.dylanwiliam.org/Dylan_Wiliams_website/Papers_files/DIMS%20%28NCME%202007%29.pdf.

Young, Toby (2014). *Prisoners of the Blob: Why Most Education Experts Are Wrong About Nearly Everything* (London: Civitas).